EVE OF DESTRUCTION

Also by Eva Shaw:

What to Do When a Loved One Dies
Divining the Future
Resumes for Women
Ghostwriting: How to Get into the Business
Writing and Selling Magazine Articles
Trade Secrets
Diana's Gift
50 Wooden Crafts to Make with Kids
60 Second Shiatzu

EVE OF DESTRUCTION

PROPHECIES, THEORIES AND PREPARATIONS FOR THE END OF THE WORLD

BY
EVA SHAW

Lowell House
Los Angeles

Contemporary Books

Chicago

Library of Congress Cataloging-in-Publication Data

Shaw, Eva, 1947-
    Eve of Destruction : prophecies, theories, and preparations for
the end of the world / by Eva Shaw.
       p. cm.
    Includes bibliographical references and index.
    ISBN 1-56565-431-5
     1. End of the world.   2. Prophecies.   3. Bible--Prophecies-
-Eschatology.   4. Forecasting.   I. Title
    BL503.S53   1995
    001.9--dc20   95-7300
                                                · CIP

Requests for such permissions should be addressed to:
Lowell House
2029 Century Park East, Suite 3290
Los Angeles, CA 90067

Lowell House books can be purchased at special discounts when ordered in bulk for
premiums and special sales. Contact Department JH at the address above.

Publisher: Jack Artenstein
General Manager, Lowell House Adult: Bud Sperry
Text design: Michele Lanci-Altomare

Manufactured in the United States of America
10 9 8 7 6 5 4 3 2 1

To the Goddess and the God of our universe:
You alone know when or if it will end.

CONTENTS

ACKNOWLEDGMENTS

This book has been made possible because many have listened, encouraged, helped and assisted. Thank you all.

Special thanks to my editor, Bud Sperry, who has performed many a miracle with the manuscript. I'm indebted to his enormous sense of humor, sensitivity and ability to direct me and the project with the finesse of a symphony conductor.

My everlasting gratitude to Joe and Matt (and Zip and Ford, too) for their unconditional support and love. They encouraged me and provided an atmosphere where doom and gloom could be balanced with laughter, kindness and hope for the future.

INTRODUCTION

GRIST FROM THE LAST DAYS' RUMOR MILLS

The End is here. Doomsday is upon us. We'd better be ready to get out. Everything points to the End. Or does it?

The millennium, also known as D day, End Times, Doomsday, the Rapture, the Apocalypse or simply the End, is the belief that the end of the world is at hand or will happen within a determinate period of time. According to many, these are the days considered to be the Eve of Destruction.

Watching the evening news seems to verify that assumption. There are killer hurricanes, abhorrent famines and breath-catching wars. There are worldwide epidemics of incurable diseases that threaten to touch almost every household. Not too long ago, we watched the news in grievous awe as most of the Midwest incurred monster floods that obliterated scores of people and animals, houses and towns and swept entire cities from the map. Californians are reminded each month, each week and sometimes every day, of the dangerous game humanity plays in earthquake roulette, San Andreas Fault–style. Recently, South Dakota experienced freezing temperatures in the summer while other parts of the country suffered from year-long droughts, deadly tornadoes and heat waves that produced record highs and immeasurable crop damage. And then there are the "killer" bees, buzzing their way ever closer to metropolitan areas of the country, unleashing havoc and fear.

Looking further, we see an unprecedented rise in street-gang warfare. It is all too common that along with pencils and papers, guns and knives are being carried into the classrooms across the nation. Every day, it seems we read of children murdering children and gang members performing executions.

The horror never takes a holiday. Brutally deformed babies are born within sight of toxic dumps. Countless men, women and children are homeless and starving within the opulence of great cities. And if this weren't enough, the delicate ecosystem of the world's rainforests, with their millions of acres of irreplaceable oxygen-producing flora, are being stripped of vegetation. Far more damage is being done to our planet's people and environment than can be repaired. Ever.

The grim pictures of now—of the days in which we live—are everywhere, from MTV and CNN to *U.S. News and World Report* and *People*. Even optimists have to agree that we live in the most trying of times. Sometimes it seems it just can't get worse—but then it does. The skeptics have cause to wonder if these reports are evidence that the Doomsday prophets are right.

Not everyone is awestruck by the idea of the End. Some people are disbelievers. Others live in fear, seeing signs of potential D day in every calamity.

For another segment of the world's population, the dire news blasting from the television is cause for a celebration of sorts. These are not the misfits of society. Rather, they are those who believe in their hearts that Jesus Christ will return at the End; they believe we are exactly at that point. One must honor these steadfast convictions. They see the inhumanity of today's events as proof of those chapters and verses of the Bible that predict the End. They like to expound on the belief that these terrible times have been preordained. "This is to be expected," they say. "This has been foretold in the Bible. These are the exact signs that Saint John wrote about to forewarn us that the End is coming." Others believe space aliens or superconscious powers will arrive instead of the Son of God.

According to self-professed experts on the End, the scenario goes something like this: After the shocking and deplorable events of the Apocalypse, the devil (Antichrist or various other evil gods) will be defeated and sinister forces will be obliterated. Of course, this will not happen without heroic and vicious battles; the identities of those who are involved and those who save the day vary from one soothsayer to the next.

After the End's catastrophic events, a new world will awaken. Most predict that in the "after days" supreme love will be everywhere. After the End, "Have a nice day" might not be just a meaningless cliché but a global slogan.

For those who predict the End—often describing in hideous detail what happens to sinners or disbelievers on Judgment Day— the "new world" concept provides hope. Those who survive the final holocaust will reside in a world preferable to our wildest fantasies (perhaps a combination of winning a million-dollar jackpot in Vegas and going to a high-school reunion in the same size clothing as worn on graduation day). It will be pollution-free, inexhaustibly fertile and brimming with virtue and harmony.

Common to all groups is the myth of a riotous finale, great suffering and fear. As the drama unfolds, two extraordinarily powerful antagonists circle in an intense battle. Eventually, evil is defeated, and there is paradise for a thousand years before the final judgment takes place.

Even before recorded time, there were groups in the world who believed that in some future period there would be a kingdom ruled by God (a divine being, the Messiah, a Christ or an appointed supervisor). This myth crosses all cultural boundaries— many others besides today's born-again Christians have believed in the End. Although the evidence in some cases is extremely sparse, it appears that the Guarani of South America, the Aztecs of

Mexico, the Karen of Burma, the Lakali of the island of New Britain and the Native Americans of the Pacific Northwest had rituals and rites relating to millennarianism.

Spiritual leaders have always prophesied the End, with plenty of explicit details that have brought many a former skeptic to his or her knees. Commonly called Doomsday, this period has been forecast since well before the writings of the Bible, although even the Bible contains disputes about the exact time and way the End will come. For Christians, the End is chronicled in the Old Testament's word of Moses and in the New Testament's Book of Revelation, with interpretation by today's biblical teachers. For New Agers, it's seen in the works of various prophets, including Nostradamus, Alice Bailey and Jeane Dixon. Buddhists await the new spiritual leader Maitreya, who will sweep in at the height of the catastrophes of this coming age. Hindu tradition implies that we are approaching Pralaya, or Doomsday, which is believed to come at the end of Kali, the final and worst of four eras, known as yugas.

Nostradamus, believed by many to be the greatest prophet ever to have lived, chronicled the End in his journals, which included dates and times arrived at through occult practices. More recently, television and radio evangelists have predicted the dates of the End. (Alas, some authors have found it necessary to change their forecast with each reprinting of their books.)

Philosophers and theorists who study Doomsday prophets, sects and cults believe that as we approach the year 2000 and the years that follow, speculation on the End will become more passionate. Why the fascination with the end of the world? This obsession is more than a personal curiosity for a great many people. Anthropologists and other scholars explain that the greater a society's problems (crime, violence, obscenity, poverty, disease, breakdown of the family unit, civil atrocities, war), the more concerned a population becomes with the End, taking solace in the belief that once this agonizing time passes, they will have deliverance in glorious nirvana, a genuine Shangri-la. So they manage to cope, believing that in their next existence, life will be less painful.

When will the End come? When is Doomsday? Will anyone survive to tell about it? More important, *will* it come? Does anyone really have special knowledge?

In the past, entire communities and vast cults have sold their worldly goods, given their money to churches, thrown their possessions into fires or the sea and stopped planting crops in preparation for an End they thought was immediately forthcoming. Today most scientists, theologians and students of history who look at Doomsday do so with a sense of intrigue. You'll have to make up your own mind on this serious, soul-searching topic. For many people, clues from the past provide a framework for the future. Doomsday is presented here in a manner to spark controversy, aid in theoretical discussions and challenge one's intellect.

This book investigates a complete range of Doomsday topics, including how people live and function in the Eve of Destruction and how the End will be brought about by pollution, the AIDS epidemic and nuclear winter. It recounts the gentle coming of the Lord, or supreme being, as predicted in some of the ancient books and tablets, and the more recent channeled prophecies. Also included are the Fundamentalist ideas of the Rapture, said to be on its way in the next few years, and the prediction that super aliens will intercede in the nick of time, as some UFO groups anticipate.

This is not a biblically based book but one that compares ideas from across the spectrum of Doomsday philosophies, including the prophecies of the Mormons, Hindus, Buddhists and Muslims. It addresses the beliefs of New Agers who channel information from the spiritual beyond, as well as religious opinions and the speculations of scientists, environmentalists and philosophers.

Throughout history, people have prophesied the destruction of the earth, envisioning hellfire and brimstone, blood in the ocean, fire from the sky, typically accompanied by screaming babies and the hideous torture of souls. Jesus and the eloquent prophets of the Bible were not alone in this attention-getting approach. Confucius, Nostradamus, William Miller, Edgar Cayce, Elizabeth Clare Prophet and others have sought to determine the when and why of our demise. These oracles threw in plenty of gruesome details, guaranteed to produce repentance in the most skeptical of earthlings. Even today—right this minute—somewhere on the planet people are carrying signs and shouting, "The End is here!"

Until the End comes, conjecture is the only way to make sense out of the chaos. And yet perhaps by reviewing the past, we may be provided with a guide to future events.

Now let's begin our journey. There's a lot to know about the past, the future and the End Times, so let's get going, while there's still time.

EVE OF DESTRUCTION

Somewhere the sky touches the earth,
and the name of that place is the End.
—WAKAMBA TRIBE, AFRICA

I
IN THE BEGINNING

The Virgin Mary visits a farm in Georgia. A group in Montana is stockpiling food and water and AK-47s. Cults throughout the world are committing mass suicides. Nationally known gospel leaders are converting believers by the thousands. What does this mean? Simply put: The world believes that we're winding it all up. We're in the final act of the human drama.

There have always been people who believe that in some future period, humanity's struggle for survival would end. In the final phase, there would be a kingdom ruled by God (a goddess, a divine being, the Messiah, a Christ or an appointed supervisor). And the end-of-time parable is one that crosses all cultural boundaries. It is the fundamental basis for the millennium. Throughout history, the notion of End Times has been embraced, feared and ridiculed. It is the basis for the belief of Fundamentalist Christians and other groups that we'd better get our act together.

In this chapter we'll look at the beginning of the story surrounding the End. As we move through these pages ever closer to the Eve of Destruction, we'll see how the myths are really the justification on which we, as 20th-century Americans, base our End Times beliefs. And our nightmares.

FASCINATING DOOMSDAY

Without a doubt, people are morbidly fascinated with the concept of the absolute End. As we speed toward the year 2000, this love-hate relationship is becoming steadily more intense. Why are we so captivated by something that is envisioned as so terrible and so unequivocal?

Most likely, the speculation began in the Stone Age, perhaps with a solar or lunar eclipse. The concept isn't that impossible when we consider for a moment what it may have been like to live at a time when even the most basic laws of physiology and physics, such as reproduction and gravity, were mysteries. For a cave dweller, dependent on the sun for warmth and light, seeing the bright sphere suddenly darken and "hide" was cause for hysteria. Even when the sun returned minutes later, the frightful possibility that it would happen again remained. Not only primitive people but also many early civilizations believed the sun might disappear one day, never to shine again, and thus the world would end.

In an attempt to appease the sun so it wouldn't "die" or "leave", they offered sacrifices. The sun (or various sun deities) was offered valuable objects—human hearts, flowers, corn, specially prepared feasts and sometimes large groups of people and/or herds of animals. No sooner had people conceptualized the End than they were trying to figure out ways to postpone it.

Logically, it follows that if there was a beginning in the far distant past, before anyone can even remember, then there must be an End in the future. If one could somehow identify the events that foretell the End or know which clues point to its arrival, perhaps preparations could be made. Anthropologists tell us that when a civilization, a community or a tribe reaches its limits of size in relation to sufficient food or shelter, millennarian movements begin to develop. As the group's situation becomes more difficult, such movements flourish. This pattern usually occurs several generations before the dynastic collapse.

Norman Cohn, author of *In Pursuit of the Millennium*, wrote, "People were always on the watch for the 'signs' which, according to the prophetic tradition, were to herald and accompany the final 'time of troubles'; and since the 'signs' included bad rulers, civil discord, war, drought, famine, plague, comets, sudden deaths of prominent persons and an increase in general sinfulness, there was never any difficulty about finding them." The threat of invasion and war is a constant throughout history. The Huns, Magyars, Mongols, Saracens and Turks all revived memories of the hordes of the Antichrist, the people of Gog and Magog who invade the towns and cities of antiquity. Cohn writes, "Above all, any ruler who could be regarded as a tyrant was apt to take on the features of Antichrist."

The *Epic of Gilgamesh*, a Babylonian epic poem chiefly known from twelve tablets of the seventh century B.C., depicts the hero, Gilgamesh, as a ruler of the first dynasty of Uruk. He is a demi-god who rules tyrannically. In the account, elaborated by the immortal Utnapishtim for the edification of Gilgamesh there is a great flood and a cleansing of the earth.

There are many similarities between the stories of Gilgamesh and Noah's ark—the use of bitumen to make the ark water-tight, the grounding of the ark on the mountain, the preservation of only a few; the gods' smelling goodly savour of sacrifice—which collectively indicate that the Bible's account is dependent on this epic or that the similarities are derived from a common root, probably an ancient Oriental mythology, the source of which has been lost in time.

The Persians, too, were concerned with the End. In the ancient texts of the Persians we find that they've embraced all the color (earthquakes, fires, floods, pestilence) found in other Doomsday prophecies and books, including those of the Bible. However, in the Persians' version of the End, there is a new twist on the plot. Here there is no new beginning, no period of grace, no beautiful beyond to give believers a sense of hope. Rather, the ancient Persians believed that Doomsday, like Creation, would only happen once. After the great battle between good and evil, called "The War of the Sons of Light with the Sons of Darkness," all humanity would be judged. The pure would go to heaven and the immoral would go in the opposite direction. The End would be an eternal status quo. The ancient Persian myths seem to have been the basis for some of the pre-Christian ideas regarding Doomsday. Some scholars suggest that they may have been the origin of the heaven and hell concepts that we still consider plausible.

The end-of-the-world myth probably originated with the ancient Hindus, then was mixed with a smattering of Persian folklore. According to Hindu legend, the universe is controlled by the goddess Kali, and its eras run in cycles. Each creative era is divided into four yugas, or ages: Satya, Treta, Dvapara and Kali. Kali is the time of the End, when the Mother turns destroyer because the race of men has become uncontrollably evil and sin is rampant. In the ancient text of the *Mahanirvanatantra*, we are told that "Due to the limited intelligence and lust of men in the Kali Yuga, they will be unable to recognize women as manifestations of the Shakti [the great mother goddess]." Only a few will understand and be able to escape spiritual degeneration. Those who do will be the devoted ones and faithful "to the lotus of their mothers' feet and to their own wives."

The Hindu text explains that Doomsday will arrive in the future. When it comes, the gods will slay each other, the earth will be covered with fire and flood, and the goddess will swallow everything. There will be nothing but chaos, a universe without form. The *Mahanirvanatantra* says, "She devours all existence," and that after a period which cannot be called time, since she has also destroyed that, Kali gives birth to a new universe.

The Puranas Sanskrit scriptures, composed in verse between the 4th and 16th centuries A.D., forecast the End much as the Bible does, providing rich examples of the evil that human beings will bring on themselves. In *Three Ways of Asian Wisdom*, author Nancy Ross recounts the Puranas' warnings:

> "There is no one, any more, in whom enlightening goodness (sattva) prevails; no real wise man, no saint, no one uttering truth and standing by his sacred word. The seemingly holy Brahmin is no better than a fool. Old people, destitute of the true wisdom of old age, try to behave like the young, and the young lack the candor of youth. The social classes have lost their distinguishing, dignifying virtues . . . The will to rise to supreme heights has failed; the bonds of sympathy and love have dissolved; narrow egotism rules . . . When this calamity has befallen once harmoniously ordered City of Man, the substance of the world-organism have deteriorated beyond salvage, and the universe is ripe for dissolution."

In the Vishnu Purana, the world finally reaches the point where "property confers rank, wealth becomes the only source of virtue, passion the sole bond of union between husband and wife, falsehood the source of success in life, sex the only means of enjoyment, and when outer trappings are confused with inner religion." Some people say this description sounds more like a review of a current movie or a thumbnail sketch for a tabloid television show than a chronicle of ancient wisdom. Perhaps this is why modern doomsayers find the ancient Hindu myths to be so shockingly prophetic.

According to Hindu religion, universe began when the sun, moon and planets stood in conjunction at the initial point of the ecliptic, and the End will come when they reach this point once more. Using Hindu reckoning, the present age started in 3102 B.C. The chronology of the Mesoamerican tribe of the Maya, who had a similar Doomsday accounting, began 11 years later, although there is no possible way one could have culturally affected the other.

The Hindus and the Mayans (along with the seventeenth-century prophet Nostradamus, whom we'll discuss shortly) predicted the End would come on or about May 2000, depending on the source and the interpretation. There have been lengthy discussions on the exact date. Some people believe that the ancients predicted the End will come on May 5, others insist that it is to be May 10. Some say it will happen in 2000, others say 2005.

According to the End Times theory of the Babylonian sage Berossus, "The world will burn when all the planets that now move in different courses come together in the Crab, so that they all stand in a straight line in the same sign, and . . . the future flood will take place when the same conjunction occurs in Capricorn. For the former is the constellation of the summer solstice, the latter of the winter solstice; they are the decisive signs of the zodiac, because the turning points of the year lie in them." (This refers to the conjunction of the planets, similar to the theory called The Jupiter Effect, that we'll discuss later.)

This conjunction of the planets is a concept found in myths around the world. It's in the ancient Egyptian religion of the Avesta and in Native American myths, too. There are traces of the myth in ancient Chinese sects. The Stoic philosophers also used the conjunction of the planets as their basis for Doomsday. They believed in the End that what nature has made into separate parts will be confounded into a single mass. This is the basic principle of Chaos, and an important part of Stoicism.

THE MYTH BEGINS TO MOVE

When other groups of preliterate peoples were quaking in caves in preparation for the time when the gods would destroy what the gods had created, the ancient people of Baal constructed huge temples at Baalbek, located in eastern Lebanon between the Litani and Asi rivers. The ancient Semitic peoples erected lookout stations to warn the population of the interstellar destroyer that they were sure would come.

At the time of their Babylonian exile, about six hundred years before the birth of Jesus Christ, the Hebrews took comfort in various End Times prophecies. Although they were forced to face great suffering, their sacrifices and oppression would, they believed, someday be worth it. The God of righteousness would triumph over the forces of evil, and their cause would be vindicated.

The perception of Christ as foretold in the Old Testament and other ancient religious writing may have begun in the ancient Buddhist scriptures, as Kalki Avatara, the Destroyer of Sin. This being would come from heaven and announce Doomsday. The Persians took the concept and called him the Son of Man or the Messiah. Before 170 B.C., in the ancient text of the *Book of Enoch*, the savior was referred to as Christos, the Anointed One. The prophets of the time announced that he had actually been born, performed various miracles, conducted a ministry and was gone again. The sages also said that His Second Coming was expected at any time.

The Druids and other northern European, pre-Christian groups (often referred to as pagans) may have drawn their Doomsday myths from the same origins. The Druids, who left only an oral history of their beliefs, called the End Ragnarok. They thought that the End would come when the goddess Mutspell (or Mother Curse) saw the violence of the gods of earth and the neglect for the old laws of peace and blood kinship. Mutspell, angered at the gods, would become Skadi the Destroyer. Like Kali in the Hindu tradition, she would devour the world in one great swallow.

This same myth is seen in the Irish folktale of the sibyl Babd, one of the three Fate goddesses (whom Christian priests renamed

Bridget). She told of the forthcoming wasteland with trees without fruit and seas without fish. Folklore tells us she foretold that old men would give false judgment and legislators make unjust laws; warriors would betray one another, and men would be thieves, and there would be no more virtue left in the world. Once more, these ancient myths seem to reflect the world in which we live today.

After the destruction, there would be a period, similar to the Chaos of the Stoic philosophers, of unaccountable time (since time was also to be destroyed). Finally the goddess Babd would produce the beginnings of a new human race from a primal couple called Life (the female) and Desirer-of-Life (her mate).

THE END AS FORETOLD
IN THE PYRAMIDS

The great pyramids of Egypt have been a mystery for thousands of years. Egyptologists agree that they hold incredible secrets from the most ancient times. Some Millennarians, as those who believe in the Second Coming of Christ are known, think they hold the secrets to the End and that all significant forthcoming events have been etched within the stone structure. The Great Pyramid at Giza is often identified as the key to ultimate knowledge, the path to human understanding of the great scheme. The monument is sometimes referred to as the Bible in stone.

Historians tell us that the Great Pyramid was built for the pharaoh Khufu (Cheops), who lived about 2575 B.C. The structure stands on 13 square acres atop the Giza Plateau. It is three miles southwest of the city of Cairo, on the banks of the Nile River. Historians and scholars have long held that the pyramid was simply a tomb for a great king.

Other groups, including some Christian sects, insist that the pyramid was standing a millennium before Khufu's time. There are rambling but intriguing theories, impossible to prove, that it was built by Atlantean architects or by technologically advanced aliens, a race of superhuman beings, or by God's own hand. Advocates of the New Age theory of pyramid power (a psychic generation of special vibrations and energy found when a person sits within or an object is placed within a pyramid shape) state that the building is an architectural, engineering and construction feat with great supernatural power. They point out that there has never been a truly exact duplicate. This group reminds doubters that the pyramid holds an astronomical calendar and observatory, a historical data bank of the beliefs of the ancient Egyptians and a place for prophetic or psychic blueprints to be kept. It is much more than a simple burial site.

Within the Great Pyramid are many passageways and shafts, which Egyptologists believe were designed to foil would-be looters seeking the riches often buried with nobility. Others believe the pyramid's design represents a calendar to the End and that the small shaft leading upward within the temple isn't a passage but a symbol of the Old Testament referring to the law of God and the prophets.

Some pyramidologists and Christian sects believe that each compartment in the maze-like structure represents God's plan for humanity. For example, it is said that the place where the shaft opens up to a high ceiling represents Christ's crucifixion. The Grand Gallery of the pyramid is said to symbolize the age of grace, when He will reign on the earth. The access to the Queen's Chamber from the Grand Gallery indicates that the church is divine. But more is in store in the stone for the believer of the End:

* There is a low doorway at the very top of the gallery. This is said to represent the great tribulation.
* The King's Chamber is believed to represent the Second Coming of Christ and the millennium.
* The pit beneath the pyramid represents hell.

* The broad pathway leading to the pit is, of course, the pathway to hell.

* The small well shaft that leads from the descending shaft to the Grand Gallery is salvation, or the way to escape from hell.

* The capstone—the top portion of the pyramid—is missing at Giza. Pyramidologists believe this signifies that the pyramid is awaiting a sculpture of Christ to be put in place on His return. Egyptologists explain that when the pyramid was built, it had a capstone just as all other pyramids did. However, sometime after construction was complete, it was probably destroyed, stolen or lost to erosion.

Pyramidologists and the Christians who see the pyramid as a bible in stone measure the structure in various complex ways to show that events since its construction prove it is the future set in stone. A typical theory is that one must measure the distance from the alleged crucifixion point in the King's Chamber (however, most disagree on whether an inch equals a year or if there is another measurement that should be used). There are pyramidologists who swear that they have found references to the Great Depression, World Wars I and II, space travel and Doomsday through the use of their measuring tape. Though it is interesting to note these theories, one does wonder why an inch would be the appropriate unit of measure rather than one used by the Egyptians or the superaliens who supposedly built the pyramids.

Does the Great Pyramid at Giza really reveal important dates and events? Charles Taze Russell, founder of the Jehovah's Witnesses, believed so. He based one of his most profound End Times theories on the stone monument's dimensions, and from this beginning gathered millions of followers worldwide.

William M. Alnor, author of *Soothsayers of the Second Advent*, says that, "by working with figures enough, one can get the Great Pyramid—or any other structure—to reveal any date one wants it to reveal." For instance, if one multiplies 42 (the age Elvis Presley was when he died) by 3 and adds 1874, the birth year of the poet Robert Frost, we can calculate the End at 2000 A.D.

Yet, New Age theorists believe there is a power contained in the Great Pyramid at Giza that is found nowhere else on earth. They believe that just sitting within a pyramid allows one to be connected to spiritual energies. If a pyramid could be built with exactly the same proportions as Giza, the energy would be incredibly powerful. If tapped into this force, one can psychically channel information about forthcoming events, including the End, and receive interplanetary communications, possibly from those who built the great structures.

ON ANOTHER SIDE OF THE GLOBE

The ancient Aztecs, with their highly organized civilization, took the End as seriously as did the early Christians. They believed they must show their devotion to the gods to keep the world humming along and that their gods wanted human sacrifices.

Like other ancient tribes, they surmised that their actions had a direct effect on whether they'd live or die and on the approach of Doomsday. Using astrological and astronomical calculations, the Aztecs came up with two distinct calendars for the cycle of life as they saw it. One was based on the solar year of 365 days. The other involved a 260-day ritual cycle. On each calendar, every day had a name, and it took 18,980 days, or about 52 years, to run through all the possible pairs.

Dr. E. C. Krupp, astronomer and director of the Griffith Observatory in Los Angeles, explains that "for the Aztecs, this 52-year cycle clicked along like an odometer to catastrophe. After both calendars returned to the same pair of dates with which the cycle had begun, the Aztecs bundled up another package of 52 years." At this interval, they performed the New Fire Ceremony—also called the Binding of Years. The ceremony entailed bundling 52 pieces of reed and burning them, symbolizing the completion of the cycle. But they didn't just burn, watch and heave a priestly sigh of relief. They agonized over the movement of the stars in the heavens, especially the star cluster of Pleiades. Their 52-year cycle ended when the calendars came together and when Pleiades could be seen. They believed that if the stars didn't move, the End would come immediately. It was such a great worry that they attempted to alter fate through intricate rituals of human sacrifice.

In Mexico, by mid-November every year, the star cluster Pleiades (seen even without a telescope as a dipperlike shape with nine bright stars) can be seen directly overhead. It was viewed by the priests and holy astronomers from a ritual temple situated on a hill near Mexico City. (The temple is now called Cerro del la Estrella, Hill of the Star.) It was here that the Aztec priests watched the Pleiades transit at midnight. It was here that they worried about the End and did their level best to appease the gods in order to ensure another 52-year cycle.

Father Bernardino de Sahagun was a Roman Catholic priest who accompanied the Spanish soldiers to Mexico in 1521. He was the first to chronicle the ancient Aztec beliefs while there were still a few Aztecs left. He wrote about the precautions taken by the Aztecs to prevent the End and the ways they kept the sun satisfied. According to Father de Sahagun, the priests and citizens put out all the fires in the city, from the smallest cooking stoves to the largest hearths. There were daylong vigils and prayer processions to the Hill of the Star. Reaching the temple, the priests prepared the human sacrifice and the New Fire Ceremony was readied.

After monitoring the movement of Pleiades (and assuming that it continued to move down to the west by early dawn), the priests began a celebration and ritual. They had been saved from doom, and the sun god was satisfied but now needed to be honored. They began to ignite the fires. (It's thought they believed that by their putting out all the fires and extinguishing any light, the sun would be forced, or see the need, to return. Yet, it is unclear why they chose this particular star cluster to determine their fate regarding Doomsday.)

Beginning the ritual of thanksgiving, the priests used fire sticks. The first fire to be lighted was on the sacrificial victim's chest. Then his heart would be cut from his chest with a flint knife and burned in a ceremonial urn or on a special rock. From this fire, torches were lighted and the "new" fire was transported down from the temple, and used to light fires in other buildings and eventually every home. Astronomers tell us that the imagery of the fire ceremony and the Aztec belief that it was their destiny to sustain the sun suggests their intent was to reignite the sun as it traveled through the dark underworld.

It remains a mystery whether the Aztecs ever calculated a time when putting out the fires of the city *wouldn't* encourage the sun to return. In a rough reckoning of the Aztec system of the End, if one calculates the 52-year cycle, the priests would be climbing the hillside and preparing the sacrifice in 2019. However, for the Aztec civilization, the End came when the conquistadors invaded and killed most of their population (they were on a quest to spread Christianity to the world, and following an End Times scenario).

For the Aztecs who were left after the massacre, it became a crime to practice the New Fire ceremony and other "heathen" beliefs. It became a crime to practice anything but Christianity. Most of the Aztecs were massacred by the early 1500s. Their myths would have died with them were it not for Father de Sahagun, who made the accounts that have kept the myths alive for historians of today. Actually, the Spanish soldiers attempted to destroy the legends recorded by the priest, but Father de

Sahagun, anticipating their savagery, duplicated his logs and hid them for posterity.

Another star-based prediction comes from the ancient Mayan calendar stone and was recently interpreted by Jose Arguelles, author of *The Mayan Factor*. According to Arguelles's interpretation, the ancient stone of the Mesoamerican tribe, Hopi prophecies and the Aztec calendar all point to the same thing at the same time: A new world is coming, because this one is rushing to a close.

Arguelles believes that the Mayan calendar, or Tzolkin, describes a 5,200-year Great Cycle. The cycle began in 3113 B.C. and will end in 2012 A.D., says Arguelles, an art historian and New Age minister. The cycle is part of another 26,000-year cycle, composed of five even greater cycles. This cycle corresponds exactly to the 26,000-year cycle in Plato's Great Year. It also happens to be the cycle of the astrological precession of the zodiac. Is it a coincidence that the great cycles also end in 2012? Many don't believe that for a nanosecond.

Arguelles says, "What we are experiencing is the climax of our particular species and evolutionary stage—the very last 26 years of a cycle some 26,000 years in length!" After the fateful year of 2012, Arguelles predicts a Solar Age, a utopia of love.

In the next chapter, we'll examine the prophecies of the End as they are foretold in the Bible. There are many details of the End that are amazingly clear today, in the twentieth century. Is the Bible a guide or the ultimate Doomsday chronicle? Stay close; we're about to take a trip back through religious history in order to see if the End is coming *now*.

Blessed is he that readeth,
and they that hear the word of this prophecy...
for the time is at hand.
—THE REVELATION OF SAINT JOHN THE DIVINE 1:3.

2
THE BIBLE: THE ULTIMATE DOOMSDAY BOOK

Is the Bible the ultimate Doomsday book? With the ferocious warnings in the Book of Revelation, it often seems that way. Can we learn what lies ahead from the Scriptures? Some folks say yes. Many believe that through the words of the ancient prophets we can find evidence that our time is up. Through the divinely inspired words, we can see the true signs to the End.

It often seems that those who wrote the Bible had all the answers, especially regarding the how and when of the End. They believed they foretold the future through their visions and the

words of God. And Jesus Christ or other God sources personally
directed St. John the Evangelist as he dramatically documented the
Tribulations in the Book of Revelation.

In the years after Jesus's ministry, crucifixion, death and
resurrection, His disciples believed that He would return within
their lifetime. The world would surely end then, because He would
rule the planet. In this chapter, we'll discuss the End from a
biblical perspective. We'll attempt to unravel some of the mystery
shrouding the ancient prophecies of early Christianity.

THE FORECASTS OF OLD

The Old Testament of the Bible, though not the first holy
record to inform humanity of its doom, provides an early Christian
reference to Doomsday. "Go thou thy way till the end be: for thou
shalt rest, and stand in thy lot at the end of the days," says the
Book of Daniel.

In the Book of Mark, Jesus infers that He is the Anointed
One, the one whose presence is foretold and who will arrive before
the planet is cleansed, as was done in the time of Noah. He is the
one who is seen "Coming in the clouds with great power and glory.
And then shall He send his angels, and shall gather together His
elect from the four winds, from the uttermost part of the earth to
the uttermost parts of heaven" (Mark 13:26-27).

However, Jesus wasn't the first or the last to believe He was
the long-awaited Messiah. The historian Josephus, writing before 70
A.D., said there were countless people who claimed that they were
the Messiah and the true Christ. These men and women traveled
through the cities, towns and countryside, announcing that the End
was near and that the population must listen to their teachings.

In Jesus's own lifetime, He warned that the End Times were
looming. "There be some standing here, which shall not taste

death, till they see the kingdom of God," he is quoted in Luke. Modern theologians often interpret this quote in a general, figurative way, that one who believes in and accepts Christ into his or her life will never spiritually perish.

It was such a certainty that the End was about to be realized, especially if the Anointed One said so, that the early teachers cautioned priests not to marry (thus the beginning of the Catholic church's renunciation of marriage and parenthood for priests and nuns) and for women to abstain from intercourse in order not to conceive. It was believed that the trials and tribulations of the final days would be so terrible that labor and motherhood would be out of the question. So strong was this admonition that Luke (21:23) wrote: "Woe unto them that are with child, and to them that give suck, in those days!"

BIBLE BOMBSHELLS OR EMPTY WARNINGS?

Most Westerners, regardless of their spiritual orientation, have some acquaintance with millenarianism gleaned from the myths of the Persians, the Hindus and the Christians. They are familiar with the belief in the Second Coming of Christ, when He will reign upon the earth in a kingdom of His saints. At the millennium's conclusion, a thousand years after its beginning, the saints will follow Him back to heaven. This is a Christian adaptation of the concepts formatted for a messianic kingdom on earth, popular in the late pre-Christian Jewish apocalyptic speculation, outlined in Daniel and the non-canonical *Book of Enoch*. It is the literal interpretation of Revelation, the final book of the Bible's New Testament that has often scared the bejesus out of various sects, cults and Fundamentalist Christian followers. This message from nearly two thousand years ago continues to speak to society today, as we approach what just may really be the end.

The Book of Revelation is rich in symbolism and may be appreciated for the poetry of its words. However, it's better known for giving humanity messages about the future. This part of the Bible is sometimes referred to as the Apocalypse, derived from the Greek *apokalyptein*, meaning "to uncover."

The author of the most quoted part of the book that heralds the End tells "sinners" what will happen if they ignore his words. Most of the secular community believes it was written by St. John the Evangelist. However, some biblical scholars now doubt that assumption, claiming that the linguistic differences between Revelation and the Gospel of John indicate they could not have been written by the same person. F. L. Cross, editor of the *Oxford Dictionary of the Christian Church*, explains that it is the consensus of biblical scholars that John didn't write Revelation since "nowhere [does John] claim to be an eye-witness of the Incarnate Christ and refers to the twelve Apostles in a reverential and detached manner (21:14) makes it improbable that he was John the son of Zabedee. It seems reasonable to suppose that the author's real name was indeed John, and that he was an otherwise unknown Christian of Jewish descent living in Asia Minor." This supposition rather throws the merit and credibility of the words into a jumble. For critics of Revelation, it also provides the basis for doubt about the reliability of the End Times prophecies.

If one assumes the traditional authorship, then it was supposedly written when John, an apostle of Jesus, was exiled to Patmos, a small, rocky island in the Aegean Sea. John had been banished there "on account of the word of God and testimony of Jesus" (1.9). John knew he had important work to do, but there were so few people to convert to Christianity on the island that it must have been extremely frustrating. Sometime during the reign of the Roman emperor Vespasian (69-79 A.D.) or possibly the Roman emperor Domitian (81-96 A.D.), John heard the call.

How did the End Times prophecies come about? We learn that there was a "loud voice like a trumpet," which told the author to "write what you see in a book and send it to the seven churches, to Ephesus and to Smyrna and to Pergamos and to Thyatira and to Sardis and to Philadelphia and to Laodicea"(1:10-11). This he did.

Revelation was written to prepare Christians for the last intervention of God in human affairs, which followers believed would happen within months or years after the physical death of Jesus. As John translated the visions he received from heavenly sources into words, he told of the evil that stalked Christians, the terrors of Roman domination under Domitian and other ruthless monarchs and the signs of deliverance. As the incidents of abuse, murder and other acts of cruelty toward Christians grew worse, the terrible times were seen as fulfillment of the prophecy that Jesus Christ was about to return. When He returned, Christians would be freed of the tyranny; He would personally see to their protection. The good would live as saints. The bad would be punished for their brutality.

Historians point out that John wrote the visions for specific purposes: to encourage Christians to endure the terrifying final crisis and to be confident with the expectation of an imminent paradise. It is believed that he also selected a writing style that was symbolic in order to hide the message from his jailers, the enemies of the Christian church. This technique is called apocalypse, a literary form characterized by an often elaborate symbolic interpretation and prediction of events.

John didn't invent this melodramatic and poetic style. It was commonly used in other Christian writing, including the Old Testament. John's contemporaries were probably more used to it than we are.

Many Christians believe we must accept the words of Revelation for what they are, a beautifully written commentary of John's time, of the pageantry of good against evil, of the visions of the Savior and of God and the final paradise. Other Christians seek hidden meanings in the pages or interpret the horrors literally, believing that the Scriptures are true predictions of the future and ignoring the Bible's own warning not to be concerned with predicting the End from the verses of Revelation. Either way, it is important to keep in mind that the exact meaning of John's words may have been distorted or lost altogether through time and various translations.

THE FUTURE FROM WORDS OF THE PAST

In order to understand future events, it is often helpful to review the past. In the case of Doomsday, the Bible prophecies written nearly two thousand years ago may help us understand why many believe that time is up. Apologies if necessary to biblical scholars—no misrepresentation or disrespect is meant. Here's a *TV Guide* version of the Book of Revelation.

John the Evangelist (or an unknown author named John or a cumulative Christian group writing in John's name—perhaps we'll never really know the truth) is told by God to write letters to the "Seven churches of Asia" to tell them of the end. The rest of the book consists of the visions John had of what was about to happen.

In the first vision, John sees the glory of God. "I looked and beyond, a door was opened in heaven and the first voice which I heard was as it were of a trumpet talking with me; which said, Come up hither, and I will show thee things which must be hereafter"(Rev. 4:1). And John told of the worshiping of the 24 elders and four winged beasts around the throne of Jesus (4).

"And I saw in the right hand of Him that sat on the throne a book written within and on the backside, sealed with seven seals"(Rev. 5:1). This book, according to John, was not available to any mortal or any angel but could only be opened by Christ (5).

As the first seal begins to open, the four infamous Horsemen of the Apocalypse appear. They tell of great earthquakes and the blackening of the sun like rough black cloth and the full moon becoming red like blood. In this portion, the stars in the sky fall to earth like figs from a fig tree when the wind blows. The sky disappears and rolls up like a scroll, and every mountain and island is moved from its place. The vision goes on to tell of people hiding in caves; regardless of their station in life, kings and slaves alike hide and call to the mountains and rocks: "Fall on us. Hide us from the face of the One who sits on the throne. Hide us from the anger of the Lamb! The great day for their anger has come. Who can stand against it?"(6).

At this time the 144,000 faithful of the 12 tribes of Israel are seen. John writes that God tells the angels who are standing at the four corners of the earth and holding the winds, "Do not harm the land or the sea or the trees before we put the sign on the people who serve our God. We must put the sign on their foreheads." John tells of the numbers from every family group of Israel (7).

As John sees this sight, great crowds surround God and John is told about how the redemption will take place. An elder tells him, "These are the people who have come out of the great suffering. They have washed their robes with the blood of the Lamb. Now they are clean and white" (7:14). And then he says they needn't be afraid any longer. "They will never be hungry again. They will never be thirsty again. The sun will not hurt them. No heat will burn them. For the Lamb at the center of the throne will be their shepherd. He will lead them to springs of water that give life. And God will wipe away every tear from their eyes" (8).

As the seventh seal beings to open, a series of seven angelic trumpets call, heralding various other terrible disasters (8). With the first trumpet, John tells of seeing hail and fire mixed with blood poured down on the earth. A third of the earth and all of the green grass and a third of the trees are burned. With the second trumpet, the mountains catch on fire and a third of the sea becomes blood, a third of the living things in the sea are wrecked, and a third of the ships are destroyed. The third angel blows the trumpet and foretells of a large star falling from the sky and polluting the streams and rivers with bitterness and of people dying from drinking the water. As the fourth trumpet is heard, a third of the sun and a third of the moon and a third of the stars are struck and become dark. A third of the day becomes dark, too. An angel streaks from the sky: Trouble! Trouble! Trouble for those who live on the earth! The trouble will begin with the sound of the trumpets that the other three angels are about to blow.

The visions of John continue with the fifth angel's trumpeting, and he sees a star fall to earth and into a deep hole. From the hole comes smoke, then the terrible locust, then power of deadly, people-torturing scorpions. The scorpions can harm only the people who do not have the sign of God on their foreheads. John sees a great army of more than 200 million horses and riders. Their breastplates are fiery red, dark blue and yellow like sulfur. The heads of the horses look like lions, with fire, smoke and sulfur coming from their mouths. They kill a third of all the people on the earth (9). Seeing all this and more, John begins to write the letters to the churches, but the angel who is standing with one foot in the sea and another on land tells him to stop writing. John hears God's secret plan, also written in a small scroll in the angel's hand, and he is then instructed to eat the book so that he can ingest all the information and spread the knowledge of which he has been told (10).

With the sound of the seventh trumpet, there is a proclamation of the kingdom of God and of Christ (11). Then God's temple in heaven is opened and John hears thunder and sees flashes of lightning, an earthquake and a great hailstorm and tells of the time of judgment.

Then two general eschatological visions are explained in which a woman is persecuted by a dragon and a war in heaven between the angelic hosts is led by Michael and Satan (12). Then another vision appears where a beast from the sea blasphemes against God and a beast from the earth comes forward. The second beast compels all men to worship the first beast under threat of death (13).

The second beast forces all people, small and great, rich and poor, free and slave, to have a mark on their right hand or on their forehead. No one can buy or sell without this mark. This mark is the name of the beast or the number of his name. Whoever has understanding can find the meaning of the number. This requires wisdom, so the prophets tell us. "The number is the number of a man. His number is 666" (13).

According to the *Oxford Dictionary of the Christian Church*, the "666" comes to us from a type of numerology begun by the Greeks and Hebrews, in which every letter of the alphabet was believed to represent a figure as well as a sound, and every name could be represented by a number corresponding to the sum of its letters. Innumerable explanations have been given of the cryptogram 666. The most probable is that Nero Caesar is intended. In Hebrew letters and using another form of numerology, it adds up to 666 (with the form "Neron") or to 616 (with "Nero"). The number 666 is especially appropriate for the "man of sin", since each digit is one less than seven, which was considered to be the perfect number. The *Oxford Dictionary* continues, "Many ingenious attempts to refer it to such persons as Mohammed, the Pope, Napoleon or Martin Luther may be safely dismissed." This seems to also hold true of Jimmy Carter and various rock stars, including Prince and Elvis Presley.

In Revelation 14–16, the visions turn to the judgment of "Babylon the Great," followed by world judgment, described under the metaphors of harvest, the vintage and the "pouring out" of the seven vials of the wrath of God. This is also the place where the great battle of Armageddon is outlined. In 17 and 18, we read of the destruction of the city of Babylon and all that is evil, symbolically represented as a harlot "arrayed in purple and scarlet."

Then there is the "marriage-supper of Christ," who is called the Lamb (and also written as the Word of God). In the text, Christ is symbolized as the bridegroom and the earth as His bride. Christ is then seen as a warrior riding into the destruction in triumphant glory. The beast and the false prophet are destroyed in a great battle, and Satan (who is behind it all) is bound for a thousand years (this is the millennium). Finally, Satan is cast into the lake of brimstone forever (19).

As we conclude this extremely concise version of the Book of Revelation, we learn of a general resurrection and judgment of the souls, the new heaven and new earth and the new Jerusalem.

William M. Alnor points out in *Soothsayers of the Second Advent* that in their eagerness to promote their own slightly slanted prophecies and give a personal update to the Bible's forecasts, many spirited Christians (including some TV and radio evangelists, New Age prophets and a number of people who believe in UFOs) may be doing themselves a disservice, especially if they truly believe what is written in the Scriptures. In Rev. 22:18-19, John offers the following cautionary words:

> I warn everyone who hears the words of the prophecy of this book: If anyone adds anything to them, God will add to him the plagues described in this book. And if anyone takes words away from this book of prophecy, God will take away from him his share in the tree of life and in the holy city, which are described in this book.

In all honesty, most of the Scriptures are confusing to the lay person. Do we dare to interpret them as a way of explaining contemporary life? If so, are we not doing what Jesus forbade? Once more, many find themselves between a rock and a hard place when it comes to translating the text of the Bible. Others find that they must decipher it in order to chart a course in these most difficult times.

ANCIENT PROPHECIES FULFILLED ON OUR DOORSTEP

Christians who believe that the End is here are often referred to as Evangelicals or born-agains; to simplify the text, they'll be grouped here as Fundamentalists. Let's look at some of the Scriptures on which most contemporary Fundamentalists base their Last Day prophecies. These are the Scriptures, along with articulate arguments, on which the Christian End Timers justify their belief in Doomsday. Some so closely foreshadow the world we live in that it's downright scary.

In 2 Tim. 3, we read: "For men will be lovers of self, lovers of money, boastful, arrogant, revilers, disobedient of parents, ungrateful, unholy, irreconcilable, malicious, gossips, without self-control, brutal, haters of good, treacherous, reckless, conceited, lovers of pleasure rather than lovers of God."

An earful, undeniably, and the possibility of the fulfillment of this prophecy is obvious to anyone who watches television or reads the newspaper. There are "lovers of self" and "lovers of money" everywhere. Nearly every one of us knows someone we consider ungrateful, disobedient and without self-control. Anyone who has recently seen a beer commercial or looked at an advertisement for an expensive luxury automobile has seen those lovers of pleasure (and one can then theorize those beautiful people may not be lovers of God as much as they are lovers of slick foreign cars). As for the brutal and treacherous, they're as close as the drug dealers hanging outside an elementary school or the members of terrorist groups.

"For nation will make war upon nation, kingdom upon kingdom; there will be famines and earthquakes in many places. Many false prophets will rise, and will mislead many; and as lawlessness spreads, men's love for one another will grow cold" (Matt. 24). Not only Fundamentalists but anyone aware of current events can correlate this Bible prediction to these terrible times. Many point to current tragedies, from the Los Angeles and Kobe earthquakes to the strife that continues in the Middle East. As for lawlessness, it can be seen everywhere and in all forms, from graffiti tagging to white-collar crime.

Again in Luke 21:11, Jesus tells of the conditions preceding His return. This forecasting may have been done as an End Times sign to the faithful. "And there will be signs in the sun and moon and stars, and upon the earth dismay among nations, in perplexity at the roaring of the sea and the waves, men fainting from fear and the expectation of the things which are coming upon the world." Thus, the hair-raising times will, according to biblical End Timers, get a whole lot worse before the End. They are more than willing to tell anyone within earshot just how bad it will be for the nonbelievers. This specific verse is often quoted to denote how close that Doomsday clock is to striking 12 and to His coming.

In Eph. 6:12, we learn that Paul warned against the possibility of spiritual warfare near the End. Mind control, New Age thought and cult propaganda are often cited. The latest government scandal might remind one of the following passage: "For we are not contending against flesh and blood, but against the principalities, against the powers, against the world rulers of this present darkness, against the spiritual hosts of wickedness in the heavenly places." Fundamentalists use such quotes to convince followers that the End is predestined—that it has been God's plan since Adam and Eve's time in the Garden of Eden.

This text is also used to legitimize disdain for those who oppose Christian beliefs—by passing out literature of an antireligious nature, for example, or by protesting against prayer in public schools or by helping women walk through the lines of angry folks who circle abortion clinics. Many Fundamentalists see these as anti-Christian lies and a fulfillment of prophecies. Some blame the government, the media and other "intolerable" groups such as the American Civil Liberties Union, various New Age movements, Planned Parenthood, and the National Organization of Women for what they consider to be the worst sort of immorality. Fundamentalists including Hal Lindsey, author of *The Late Great Planet Earth*, say that these groups, with their anti-Jesus doctrines, are setting the stage for a potentially dangerous wave of anti-Christian persecution like we've never seen before. Anti-Christian oppression is yet another End Times prophecy being fulfilled.

According to the Fundamentalists, there are hundreds of Scriptures to substantiate that these are the years leading to the End. For instance in John 16:2, we learn, "The time is coming, when whoever kills you will think that he is doing God a service." This Scripture may allude to the unholy war and killing waged in the former Yugoslavia or the murders in Palestine and other hot spots of the world. It might refer to the drive-by shootings that horrify city dwellers. It may apply to any number of fanatics who take the law into their own hands in the name of God. It is a powerful Scripture in the hands of Christian End Time believers.

In Nah. 2:1, 3, 4, we hear how it might be on the day that Jesus Christ arrives "He that dasheth in pieces is come up . . . the chariots shall be flaming torches in the day of his preparation, and the fir trees shall be terribly shaken. The chariots shall rage in the streets, they shall jostle against one another in the broad ways: they shall seem like torches, they shall run like the lightnings." If that doesn't describe the mass exodus from a metropolitan area with cars jostling on the freeways, nothing does.

From Matt. 24:7: "In various places there will be famines. . ." And from Rev. 6:8: "And I looked, and behold, an ashen horse; and he who sat on it had the name Death; and Hades was following with him. And authority was give to them over the fourth part of the earth, to kill with sword and with famine and with pestilence and by the wild beasts of the earth." Perhaps this is the age of famine, as fundamentalist preachers, teachers and the man and woman on the street tell us, often quoting some or all of the above Scriptures to prove their argument.

SIGNS OF THE TIMES

With the devouring of the rain forest that filters and produces clean air and the widening of the holes in the ozone layer, doomsayers point out that we are surrounded with signs of the End Times. There are constant reports of overpopulation, hostile governments, inept and dangerous bureaucracies and drastic changes in the weather. Worldwide famine is on the rise.

We've all seen the photos of marines trying to escort food to Somalians on the brink of starvation. There were children so emaciated that some of us turned away in pain. But according to Marc Cohen, [author of a paper called "Hunger 1993" (produced for the Bread of the World Institute) and] an expert on global famine, "Somalia is a drop in the bucket. It is estimated that 5.5 billion humans are suffering from malnutrition, from the acute to the marginal." This gruesome statistic does not include those with 'hidden hunger,' such as the babies and toddlers we see neglected by parents who are addicted to drugs or alcohol. In these End Times, say the Fundamentalists, it's all in the Bible—along with just what will happen next.

Luke 21:11 tells of the events leading to D day, including the spread of incurable diseases: "And there will be. . .in various places plagues. . ." Was the devastation of AIDS, flesh-eating bacterial infections, superstrong tuberculosis germs, widespread cholera and other diseases predicted two thousand years ago? If it's true, as some Fundamentalists say it is, then why isn't it also possible that the Bible prophets accurately predicted the End?

According to the AIDS Center at Harvard University, as many as 110 million people throughout the world will be infected with the AIDS virus by the year 2000. [In an article from *International Healthwatch Report* (May-June 1992),] Dr. Johnathan Mann, director of the International AIDS Center, said, "The pandemic is spreading to new areas and new communities. The disease has not peaked in any country and will reach every country by the end of the century because governments and international organizations lack effective means to control it."

The Fundamentalists explain that there are other plagues, too, that have nothing to do with the sickness of the body. There are plagues of locusts, killer bees and rodents taking over the cities as well as the suburbs of America and the world. Fundamentalists point out that the seemingly mysterious plague-like disease of hantavirus that occurred in the early 1990s in the Southwest, is simply one more sign of the End Times. Scientists who may or may not have read Luke 21:11 say there's nothing really obscure about the virus, as it's common to wildlife, but with a depletion of natural predators, the rat population has exploded. Rats carry the virus and transfer it to humans. Rats also carried the fleas that were infected with the bubonic plague that ravaged Europe in the Middle Ages.

For connections between the environment and Bible prophecies, Fundamentalists need look no further than Rev.15:9: "And men were scorched with fierce heat; and they blasphemed the name of God who has the power over these plagues; and they did not repent, so as to give Him glory." Fundamentalists tell followers that this passage refers to the holes in the ozone layer and the dangers of increased ultraviolet rays on human skin. Even daily weather reports are now giving the intensity of the sun and advising us how long it's safe to be subjected to its rays.

For those who may still be on earth when Christ returns, Fundamentalists sometimes quote Isa. 24:1, 6, which can easily be translated to read like the headlines from a nuclear war: "Below, the LORD lays the earth waste, devastates it, distorts its surfaces, and scatters its inhabitants . . . a curse devours the earth, and those who live in it are held guilty. Therefore, the inhabitants of the earth are burned, and few men are left."

PROVING THE END

Fundamentalist leaders and teachers support their various theories regarding the End by linking current events to Bible prophecies. They reflect back to the prophecies outlined in the Old Testament concerning the First Coming of Christ. Since these prophecies, written hundreds of years before Jesus's birth, were fulfilled, they are absolutely certain that the New Testament prophecies are just as legitimate.

Here are a few of the prophecies concerning Christ's First Coming, with New Testament citations following each one:

* The prophet Nathan predicted that someone from King David's ancestral line would become God's Promised One. "I will establish his throne forever. I will be his father, and he will be my son. I will never take my love away from him . . . I will set him over my house and my kingdom forever; his throne will be established forever" (1 Chron. 17: 12-14).

* Jesus was a descendant of David according to His mother's lineage (Luke 1:27). Jesus was a descendant of David also from Joseph, His earthly father (Matt. 1:6, 16).

* Jesus would be like Moses, and God would require everyone to listen to His words. "I will raise them up a Prophet from among their brethren, like unto thee, and

will put my words in his mouth; and he shall speak unto them all that I shall command him" (Deut. 18:18).

* Jesus would be born in Bethlehem. ". . .Bethlehem. . . out of thee shall he come forth unto me that is to be ruler of Israel; whose goings forth have been from of old, from everlasting" (Mic. 5:2).

* Jesus would be born of a virgin. "Therefore the Lord himself shall give you a sign; Behold, a virgin shall conceive, and bear a son, and shall call his name Immanuel" (Isa. 7:14).

* A messenger would precede Jesus Christ. "Behold, I will send my messenger, and he shall prepare the way before me: and the Lord whom ye seek, shall suddenly come to his temple, even the messenger of the covenant, whom ye delight in: behold, he shall come, saith the Lord of hosts" (Mal. 3:1).

* Jesus would come with retribution. He would open the eyes of the blind and heal the deaf, dumb and infirm and perform many miracles, including producing water in the desert. ". . .[Y]our God will come with vengeance. . .he will come and save you. Then the eyes of the blind shall be opened, and the ears of the deaf shall be unstopped. Then shall the lame man leap as an hart, and the tongue of the dumb sing: for in the wilderness hall waters break out, and stream in the desert" (Isa. 35:4-6).

* Great nations would revere Jesus. "Yea, many people and strong nations shall come to seek the Lord of hosts in Jerusalem, and to pray before the Lord" (Zech. 8:22).

* Jesus would enter Jerusalem on a beast of burden. "Rejoice greatly, O daughter of Zion; shout, O daughter of Jerusalem: behold, thy King cometh unto thee: he is

just and having salvation; lowly, and riding upon an ass, and upon a colt the foal of an ass" (Zech. 9:9).

* Jesus would be betrayed for thirty pieces of silver. "And I said unto them, If he think good, give me my porice; and if not forbear. So they weighted for my price thirty pieces of silver" (Zech. 11:12 and Psalm 41:9).

* Jesus would be beaten and die for the salvation of humanity. "But he was wounded for our transgressions, he was bruised for our iniquities: the chastisement of our peace was upon him; and with his stripes are healed" (Isa. 53:5).

* Jesus would be resurrected, and this gave followers faith in a savior. "Therefore my heart is glad, and my glory rejoiceth: my flesh also shall rest in hope. . . and at my right hand there are pleasures for evermore" (Psalm 16:9-11).

* And in Isaiah, we read that when Israel is restored to Palestine, the once-uninhabited land will blossom with flowers and the desert will become green, and Jesus will return. "The wilderness and the solitary place shall be glad for thee; and the desert shall rejoice, and blossom as the rose. It shall blossom abundantly, and rejoice even with joy and singing: the glory of Lebanon shall be given unto it the excellency of Carmel and Sharon, they shall see the glory of the Lord and the excellency of our God" (Isa. 35:1-2).

The theologian James J. Brookes, said, "Among the early Christians there was perhaps no doctrine that was more the object of firm belief, and the ground of more delightful contemplation, than that their ascended Master would return." This event was so anticipated that it is mentioned and prophesied in the Old

Testament more than five hundred times. Fundamentalists conclude that since Jesus Christ did come to save humanity, the other visions of the Bible must be true as well.

The Scriptures quoted above are only a sampling of those used by mainstream Christians as well as Fundamentalists to support their claim that the End is fast approaching. As with many religious texts, they are open to interpretation.

COMINGS AND GOINGS: THE FIRST MILLENNIUM AND EARLY CHRISTIANITY

"There are almost as many prophets of imminent doom as could ever be found in the cities of medieval Europe or the villages of modern India or Indonesia," writes Daniel Cohen in *Waiting for the Apocalypse*, "The fear—and more often the hope—that the world will come to a quick and violent end is. . .very much with us today."

The prophets who have foretold that the world would end at a specific time in our past have obviously been wrong. They were so sure that it would end, the possibility that they might be wrong didn't exist. If you're reading this, you know there has been an error in the calculations. . .at least so far. Whether they've been off by a few years or a few hundred years, only the future or the Supreme Being (depending on one's belief system) knows for sure. The future holds the secret of when or if there will be an end.

At the time of their Babylonian exile, about six hundred years before the birth of Jesus Christ, the Hebrews took solace in the belief that there would be a heaven for them. The message was also heard in the voices of the Bible prophets Daniel, Enoch, Moses and Baruch, and the heavenly concept sustained their people in the darkest of times.

Early Christians pinned their hope for a heaven on earth on the Messiah, and He was their God of the Apocalypse. Whatever hardships they were forced to bear would be justified when He returned. Historians tell us that less than two hundred years after Jesus Christ's physical death (some say only 50 years later), apocalyptic groups were flourishing wherever Christianity was preached.

A TRIP BACK IN THE DOOMSDAY TIME MACHINE

The earliest Christians believed that Christ would return within their lifetime and humanity as they knew it would end. So certain were they that it would get worse before it got better that the apostle Paul warned followers to live a celibate life.

Paul's proclamation of the End failed to come to pass at the predicted time, and in 156 A.D., or thereabouts, the Montanist movement of Phrygia (an ancient country in Asia Minor, now Turkey) began heralding the End. The leader of the group, the prophet Montanus, declared himself to be the "Spirit of Truth," an incarnation of the Holy Spirit mentioned in John's Gospel, and the Awaited One. Historians say that Montanus was a charismatic speaker, and within months of this proclamation the number of his followers ballooned.

The Montanists followed their priest through the countryside. He had been converted to Christianity, and through a divine vision had taken on the responsibility of preaching in loud, bellowing terms that humanity's days were numbered. Virgins followed him in awe, covering their faces so that no man would see them before the Bridegroom returned. Wives lived apart from their husbands, with their husbands consent, so that the Lord would find them pure. All gave up their possessions so that they'd meet their Lord empty-handed.

After renouncing all physical and worldly pleasures, Montanus's followers huddled in prayer and waited. The Montanist movement became synonymous with fasting and prayer, and the only excursions away from the caves were pilgrimages to the mountains to await the Lord. Slowly the group members splintered and formed or joined other sects. History does not note what happened to the righteous leader, but other devout leaders took his place.

Montanus predicted that the New Jerusalem would descend in what is now central Turkey within his lifetime and that it would be a paradise, a place for all saints. Although his date for D day came and went, followers continued to be committed. They gathered on hills waiting for the Second Coming. Word of the imminent arrival of Christ spread as far as Africa and Spain. So strong was belief in the End that Tertullian, the most famous theologian of the time, joined the Montanist movement.

In 431 A.D., the Catholic Church's Council of Ephesus condemned the Montanist End Times beliefs as dangerous superstition. Nonetheless, as late as the Third Crusade, some of the soldiers that marched toward the Middle East swore that they had seen the New Jerusalem hovering in the skies. They were sure that the End was fast approaching and wondering if they'd meet Jesus Christ during the campaign or when they returned home. The movement was slow to fade away; modifications of the Montanist theme resurfaced at various times.

The Crusades were actually a fulfillment of the End Times prophecies. Based on the notion that the world must convert to Christianity before the Second Coming, called postmillenialism, the church recruited the able-bodied to exterminate Jews and any non-Christian believers in order to usher the way for Christ's return.

In about 300 A.D., the Roman presbyter Novatian was called a heretic when he preached Christianity. He gained a reputation as a prophet, and Christians followed him, listening to and accepting his forecasts of Doomsday. He taught that Christ's return was imminent, the church should warn its people, and the people should get ready. Novatian attracted great crowds wherever he traveled, just like Montanus had with his Doomsday message. The followers chanted their favorite prayer: "Come, Lord Christ, clothed in all Thy wrath and judgment, come with all Thy vengeance, come."

When Novatianism faded, next came the Donatists, followers of Donatus of Africa. Donatus, among other things, told his followers that the Bible strictly limited the chosen of the Lord to 144,000. This figure supposedly indicates the inner circle John talked about in Revelations, "I looked and, lo, a Lamb stood on Mount Zion and with him a hundred and forty and four thousand, having his Father's name written in their foreheads" (Rev.14:13).

When the End did not come as predicted by Novatian, the group evolved into other sects, including the Anabaptists, Waldensians, Albigenses, Morvaian Brethren, Swiss Brethren, all apocalyptic advocates, all waiting and praying for the End. They had many things in common, chiefly that they chose to live life simply. Their theory was that if one could make it through this very difficult time, a better life was forthcoming because Jesus would return shortly. Many declared that they were ready to die for Christ and die for what they believed in. Since the groups were persecuted for their beliefs, many did die. These sects are known as the millennialists, and they include pre-millennialists and post-millennialists. Basically, pre-millennialists believe that Christ will return with His saints to establish the earth kingdom promised by David. Post-millennialists believe that Christ will return after the church has Christianized society. Though they differed on some issues, they all agreed that there was a literal heaven, a literal hell and a literal devil, whose forces were lying in wait for the day when the Antichrist would rule. They believed that there would be a great Battle of Armageddon as foretold in the Book of Revelation.

In the fourth century, St. Ambrose of Milan took up the Doomsday cause. He saw the Antichrist in the leader of the Goths, the ancient Teutonic people who had plundered the cities of Thrace, Dacia, and Asia minor and along the Aegean Coast, and ruthlessly killed and maimed. St. Ambrose warned his followers of terrible events to come and told them that Jesus Christ would return. He proclaimed to everyone and anyone who would listen that the End was surely only days away. When the event didn't occur and St. Ambrose died, his crusade faded.

Others probably pushed the Doomsday panic button after Ambrose, but little is known about their teachings until about 900 A.D., when an ecumenical council in Rome announced the last days were here. Jesus Christ would return about 1000 A.D., ushering in the Golden Age. One can imagine the effect that announcement would have today coming straight from the Vatican. Whether one is Catholic or not, one can surely see that the proclamation would cripple part of the world and inspire a lot of people to prepare to face their judgment.

Back then, if the Pope said it must be true, then it must be true. The Doomsday explosion at this time was supposedly of unprecedented magnitude. Christian scholars tell us that doomsayers of that time had much in common with those who are today screaming "The End is here." What occurred back then lacked only the media coverage. At this time the doomsday message wasn't dispersed by a group of isolated Doomsayers. Instead the claims came again from the Roman Catholic hierarchy; it was the Church that was doing the hollering and wondering what had become of us all.

As in the past when Doomsday prophecies had attracted widespread attention, great numbers of believers left their jobs, walked away from their homes, gave their money to the poor and waited.

The flip of the calendar from December 31, 999, to January 1, 1000, caused only minor ripples—or dramatic upheaval, depending on whom you consult. Some scholars have depicted dramatic scenes of citizens going berserk with the notion that the world would end and with the Pope ready to preside over a final mass. They tell of the longing for a new world, or at least the End of the ghastly old one. They sketch a picture of the world's population refusing to plant crops (why bother?), setting fire to possessions (who would need the stuff?) and refusing to work or conduct business in the normal way. Rioting is said to have resulted when the End didn't come, because there wasn't enough food. Commerce had screeched to a halt and most people had quit trying to eke out a living.

One must keep in mind, however, that few records are available to tell us what really happened in 999, and so the course of human events is up to much speculation. We do know that the world was filled with dreadful diseases, absolute poverty, rotten food and polluted water. Most Europeans huddled in dirt or straw houses, in mortal fear of marauding bandits or packs of wolves and living on the brink of starvation. If they were fortunate, the feudal landowner gave them a few coins to buy salt (a commodity controlled by the landowner) with which to preserve food so the meat wouldn't rot quite so quickly. People rarely saw their thirtieth birthdays, and death was an ever-present possibility.

During this time, there was a great shortage of workers. It was so extreme that taxes were levied on young people who didn't marry or produce children in their teens. Abortion was considered homicide, and any woman who chose to terminate a pregnancy, for any reason, was expelled from the church.

Did they fear the wrath of God or of Judgment Day? Realistically, the struggle of living from day to day may have been more than sufficient to keep their minds off heavenly thoughts. Since the majority of the world's population was illiterate, it's a good guess that few even knew about the End. For those who did understand, the alternative to living (i.e., afterlife in heaven) may have seemed mighty attractive.

Whether the masses were aware that the announcement from the Vatican had been faulty is unclear. But this didn't stop other Doomsayers from picking up the End Times torch. In the chaos of options concerning the where and when of the end, there were voices of reason. Maimonides was one of these.

Maimonides (1135-1204), also known as Moses ben Maimon and Rambam (from Rabbi Moses Ben Maimon), was one of the great Hebrew scholars. He wrote that it was not wise to expect the Messiah to prove his authenticity by performing "miracles and wonders, and create new things in the world or cause the dead to rise." Rather, the Messiah is "a human being involved in human activities, dependent upon the military expertise and ethical religious accomplishments of the nation." Jews believe that the world will continue when the true Messiah arrives, but with the addition that peace will prevail. According to the ancient Hebrew book *Laws of Government*, Chapter 11, Law 3, one can identify the coming of the true Messiah in this way: "Everything will be the same except that Israel will not be subservient to other nations," and that He will bring Israel national sovereignty and the world peace.

Many people believe that the End is quickly approaching since the Jewish nation of Israel has been restored, thus realizing the second part of Maimonides' prediction. Perhaps the next millennium will be one of world peace. Perhaps it will be the End.

In chapter 3, the world begins to awaken from the doom of the Middle Ages. With that wake-up call, Doomsday prophets spread their message: All of heaven or hell is about to break loose!

The end of the world is a point at which history,
the story of life as we know it,
intersects with eternity.
—Yuri Rubinsky and Ian Wiseman, authors of
A History of the End of the World

3

THE DARK AGES AWAKEN TO DOOMSDAY

Regardless of the details, Doomsday is always designated as a time between two distinct years or eras. In 999 A.D., as discussed in the previous chapter, the Catholic church warned that the End would come the next year. The year 2000 will, most likely, be filled with the same kinds of dire warnings and a good measure of handwringing on the part of doomsayers.

Prophets of the past followed a Doomsday timetable that was complex and open to interpretation. The millenarians' sense of time, however, is neither strictly cyclical nor is it linear. In Christian as well as Islamic traditions, the millennium is the final time, but there will be a utopia in the final act. Therefore, technically, time or history will continue. Other millenarians believe in a destructive and totally final end with no afterworld. They believe that just as there was a beginning of time, a starting point, there will be an end, a stopping point, when people and animals and everything will cease to exist on the planet.

Believers in an afterworld predict that Doomsday will be followed by a return to a carefree life (to heaven or a reward)—a release from worldly cares and a deliverance from the sorrow, oppression, agony and social cancers that presently afflict us. Such groups pin their hopes on a messiah who promises a new world.

The end of the world, according to Yuri Rubinsky and Ian Wiseman, the authors of *A History of the End of the World*, is a distinct place where history intersects with eternity. They believe the End Time scenarios of the Apocalypse and the Second Coming are not synonymous but opposite. The Second Coming is based on the premise that time never ends, and the Apocalypse is the final resolution.

Those who believe in the cyclic end of time have often postulated a new world, or for that matter, heaven on earth. This is far from a new idea. Lois Parkinson Zamora, editor of the book *The Apocalyptic Vision in America*, says Christopher Columbus, for example, quoted passages from Revelation and Isaiah in his journals that described the new heaven and new earth.

Columbus believed that his voyage was in preparation for the End. In writing to his Spanish patrons, he said, "I feel deeply within me that there, where I have said, lies the Terrestrial Paradise." His ocean quest had a purpose—to further the word of God—and the religious determination of the explorer came to light later in his years.

Like the later American colonists and the Spanish conquistadors, Columbus saw the voyages and discovery of the New World as fulfillment of biblical prophecies. It was, to him and other explorers, the anticipated scheme and the great plan of God for the End of the world.

SPREADING THE WORD OF THE END

Long before Columbus, the Third Crusade, c. 1186 to 1192, brought on new excitement about the End. Rumors, gossip, occult divination and astrological predictions foretelling the End and supposedly originating in Spain were carried back to England by the returning soldiers and their families. In late 1186, a document called the "Letter of Toledo," believed to have originated in Spain, began circulating in England and inspiring rumors throughout Europe. The letter contained a timetable to the End and as the crusading armies returned, exhorted people to hide in caves and seclude themselves and their families in the mountains. It predicted the world was about to come to a raging end, but before that conclusion, there would be hostile winds, brutal drought and a whole lot of famine, pestilence and earthquakes. Of course faithful Christians would be saved, but according to the letter, the numbers of survivors would be limited. Only a few really good Christians would make it. Yet the End never arrived.

Brother Arnold, known as a friend to the poor, predicted that the holocaust and Doomsday would occur in 1260. A dissident Dominican monk, he told followers that it was as bleak as it could be. He was all set to personally call upon Christ in heaven to ask that He respond and appear on earth to pronounce His Judgment. Brother Arnold was sure that things in the thirteenth century couldn't get any worse, so it must be the End. At the same time that Brother Arnold was visiting with Jesus, he said he would ask Christ to reveal that the Pope was the Antichrist and the clergy were limbs of the Antichrist. Poor Brother Arnold had a large following, but apparently was unable to persuade Jesus to do his bidding since He didn't respond. The movement faded, yet the End was still on the minds of many.

Martinek Hausha, a Doomsday prophet in the early 1400s, led a group of disgruntled priests in predicting that the End would come in 1420, between February 1 and 14. Hausha promised

God's wrath would be felt throughout Christendom, and that He would level every town and set fire to the villages. Hausha urged everyone to take to the mountains for safety. It is unclear whether the populace heeded his warning, but vast fires (supposedly set by Hausha and his group but which they hoped would be attributed to the Almighty) did occur. God's rage at the culture's degeneracy was never fulfilled as predicted.

Magnetic Thomas Muntzer, of Munster, Germany, and a group of followers resurrected the Montanism theories of the End that we discussed in Chapter 1. Muntzer said that the world was about to end and Jesus Christ would return shortly. Awakening from the Dark Ages, the masses sought a spiritual leader. Muntzer became that leader to the impoverished, starving peasants and led a revolt in 1525-26. As he preached to the penniless masses about D day, Muntzer was adamant that the rich and the powerful, whether Roman or Lutheran, could not be God's elect. This was not a popular stance, since the church and clergy were either rich or controlled by the rich and powerful. Muntzer had his own interpretation of the Bible. He said the Antichrist was none other than Martin Luther, called by some people of the time as the "whore of the German princes."

Muntzer contended that God had specifically spoken to him about the End Times. He insisted that he was told to rally the poor and the oppressed because the End was near. He believed that God's mission for him was to exterminate the rich. He also concluded that upon Christ's return, the downtrodden would become the saints. This prophet met the same fate as many others—an untimely, government-issued death for his cause.

In 1527, another German, Hans Nut, a bookbinder by trade, drew a large End Times following with his message of ruin. He believed that he was the Messiah outlined in the Bible. He told followers that God would arrive in 1528 and prove it to them. After He was settled on earth, everybody would enjoy free food, free love and free sex. This was a popular proposition even then. The prophecy failed when God didn't arrive. Nut was arrested by the Roman Catholic church and he was killed in an ill-fated attempt to escape prison.

A more successful group, the Anabaptists divined that the New Jerusalem would be in Munster, Germany, or France and planned the date for sometime in 1533 or 1534, when God's love would flow. Even when D day didn't arrive, followers became more zealous (this is a typical scenario, although the contrary would seem to be more logical). Two of their followers were said to be messengers of God, and a Dutch refugee became their leader. Jan Bockelson (also recorded in history as Jan Matthys) set up a New Jerusalem in Munster. Using force, he quickly expelled non-believers from inside the city's walls, including all Lutherans and Catholics. In an unusual move for Protestants and Catholics, the ousted banded together, formed an army (as mirrored in the events of Waco, Texas) and overpowered the charismatic religious leader. Bockelson's reign of terror ended with his capture by governmental forces and subsequent death, but the true End didn't come.

THE END IN A CRYSTAL BALL OR BOWL OF WATER

Not everyone at that time was preaching that the Second Coming was at hand. One prophet of Doomsday projected the end far into the future. That man was Nostradamus.

Nostradamus, the magical name of Michel de Nostre Dame (1503-1566), is known as a seer and a mystic throughout the Western world. He's a superstar among prophets, the Michael Jordan or Wayne Gretzky of the world of prophecy. Without a doubt, as we fast approach the turn of this century, we'll be hearing more about Nostradamus and the accuracy (or foolishness, depending on one's opinion) of his prophecies.

The French physician's prophecies continue to haunt, intrigue, plague, mystify and/or satisfy scholars and students of the End. His most important work, *The Centuries*, written in 1555, is still in print and referred to today. Like his other writing, this book was written in vague, poetic form, mixing French, Latin, Italian, Portuguese and Spanish along with ancient Hebrew. This wasn't done to baffle us, but rather to save his skin. Nostradamus wrote his predictions at a time of intense persecution and ruthlessness from the Catholic church. Anyone who dared to be different wasn't different for long because such people were typically hunted down and tortured or, if they were lucky, instantly killed. Well-educated and savvy to the ways of the church, the physician/psychic avoided this end by writing his prose in a tangled form of poetry.

Therefore, to protect his reputation, family, hide and life, Nostradamus wrote dramatic anagrams written in stanzas (or four lines of verse) divided into centuries. Here, the term *century* connotes the division of the work into groups of 100 four-line stanzas, or quatrains, and is not a reference to actual years. The entire book includes 354 quatrains. They are heavily symbolic, their meanings obscured and open to extensive interpretation. In some cases, the quatrains are so vague it is impossible to decipher their meanings; critics are quick to point to these verses. In others, for instance the quatrain regarding Louis Pasteur, the pioneer of immunology and microbiology, Nostradamus comments specifically on the scientist's discoveries, using the doctor's name, *333 years before his time*. This is one of the quatrains used by the prophet's boosters to show that all of the future predictions are factual. (Critics can provide no explanation for this incredible coincidence; most refuse to comment on it.)

In order to make the prophecies even less suspicious to the church, when Nostradamus finished his lengthy prognostications, some scholars speculate that he threw the pages into the air so the sequence of events would be further jumbled. Whether or not this is true, it does make for a fascinating anecdote. At any rate, only someone who was willing to invest years of study and who possessed a working vocabulary of many languages could possibly understand the scribbles. (Many Nostradamus scholars have done exactly that.)

Nostradamus came from a well-educated and wealthy family in the St. Remy de Provence area of France. He was born a Provencal Jew, but when he was a child his family converted to Catholicism. Biographers tell about his psychic visions as a child and a teenager and how he foresaw events in his own community. They say that rather than believe that the boy was possessed by the devil, his family attributed his ability to forecast the future to a divine gift. As a young man, he was a hungry and thorough scholar, delving into the languages of Hebrew, Latin and Greek as well as mathematics, medicine, astronomy, the Kabbalah and astrology. He studied medicine and received a medical degree from Montpellier University in France, but it wasn't until an outbreak of plague that his fame as a healer spread throughout France.

His healing methods were unconventional. Refusing to use leeches or other methods to bleed the dying or the infirm, he prescribed boiled water for drinking and for cleansing the body along with a score of herbs. Rosehips, a source of vitamin C, was utilized by Nostradamus and regarded by his grateful patients as a sort of wonder drug.

About 1534, Nostradamus married, fathered his first child and met his mentor, Julius Caesar Scalinger. An astrologer and philosopher, Scalinger changed Nostradamus's life. Through this friendship, Nostradamus began to investigate the study of metaphysics and make notes as to what he saw for the future.

Unfortunately, although Nostradamus could somehow foresee events well into the future and had a reputation as a miracle healer, he didn't anticipate what would become of his own loved ones. His wife and their two children died in an outbreak of plague when he was away on a medical mission in another part of France. Nostradamus grieved deeply, withdrew from society and delved more passionately into the occult and to ritual magic. In about 1550, Nostradamus remarried and fathered six more children. He settled in Salon en Craux de Provence and earnestly began recording his psychically or heavenly inspired visions.

When his book, *The Centuries*, was published in 1555, Nostradamus's fame sparked the attention of the French nobility and the rich and elite of the time. He became the pet of the French court and the personal astrologer of Catharine de' Medici, the queen of France. Legend has it that she invited him to cast the horoscopes for her sons and when Charles IX ascended to the French throne, Nostradamus not only was the court astrologer but became the court physician, too. The poor as well as the aristocracy held him in awe. When he died in 1566, he was still considered to be the greatest prophet of all time and an honor to the country of France.

Nostradamus's method for forecasting the future can be found in some of the ancient magical books, technically called Grimoires. In order to contact the spirits or to have futuristic visions, historians say, the great prophet retreated alone to his study for a long period of meditation. For hours, he would stare at a bowl filled with water placed on a brass tripod. (Some other sources insist that he stared at a shiny object such as a crystal ball; others assert that he used a mirror or even a piece of highly polished quartz.)

After considerable meditation, he supposedly touched a magic wand to the tripod, dipped the wand into the water, asked for spiritual assistance and touched the wand's tip to his robe. It was then that the visions would start. Metaphysical historians differ on whether he received voice transmission or pictures, but they do agree that Nostradamus believed the words were coming from the "Divine Presence" who "sits close."

It has been said that Nostradamus was the greatest psychic of all time. He is believed to have correctly foretold such events as the American Revolution, the Civil War, the assassination of Lincoln, both world wars and the murders of Robert and John Kennedy, as well as the rise of Hitler.

Nostradamus had quite a following in the past and his fame continues today. Much like the people who interpret the Book of Revelation, those who believe in Nostradamus's predictions point out that he predicted happenings and technology that would have been impossible to imagine when he was alive. They believe he foretold air travel, atomic and nuclear bombs, manned space flight (including the tragedy of the Challenger), rockets and submarines.

Nostradamus supporters insist that he also predicted events leading straight to the End. Generally, it is nearly impossible to pinpoint the events and catastrophes indicated in Nostradamus's work since the writing is vague, the phrases symbolic and the meanings obscure. However, this hasn't stopped the scores of people who have attempted to understand its hidden meanings. Depending on the source quoted and the translation made, Nostradamus believed the End would come from worldwide destruction sometime between June 7, 1994, and May 2000 or 2005. The prophet devotes five quatrains (or stanzas) to the sudden and violent natural occurrences that rock the planet in the spring of 2000. From the following we learn:

 C9Q83:
The sun, twenty degrees into Taurus (May 10)
There will be a tremendous earthquake,
The great theater filled will be ruined,
The air, heaven and the Earth will be dark and obscure
When the unbelievers call on God and the saints.

The prophet predicts events well into the year 8000 A.D., which is referred to as the Age of Sagittarius or Age of Truth. His translators document this forecast by the quatrain: "Some will live in Aquarius other in Cancer for a longer time." After terrible disasters, from floods to blood plagues, there will be a period of war and global destruction unlike anything we've ever known, followed by a thousand-year calm. In a letter written to his son Caesar: "Before the moon has finished her entire cycle [1889-2250], the sun [twentieth century] and then Saturn [Aquarian Age] will come. According to the celestial signs the reign of Saturn will come a second time [Capricorn Age], so that all is calculated, the world draws near to its final death-dealing cycle."

Let's peek at the past and then look into the future through some of Nostradamus's predictions written well before *The Centuries* was published. One must remember that the predictions are still open to much interpretation.

C1Q35:
The young lion will overcome the older one
On the field of combat in single battle.
He will pierce his eyes through a case of gold
Two wounds made one, then he dies a cruel death.

July 10, 1559. This quatrain is one of Nostradamus's most famous. It has become legendary as the validation of the prophecy of the accidental death of King Henry II of France. The accident happened on a thoroughfare outside of Paris. "The young lion" was Count de Montgomery, whose lance pierced the king's visor—a visor made of gold.

C10Q100:
The great empire will be for England
The all-powerful one through the sea for more than 300 years:
Great forces will pass by land and sea,
The Portuguese will not be satisfied.

1658-1961. This quatrain is believed to reflect the rise and fall of the British Empire. The prophet wrote about how it would lose great tracts of land over a two-hundred year period, more than one hundred years before the decline began.

C2Q51:
The blood of the just will be demanded of London
Burnt by fire in the year '66
The ancient lady will fall from her high place,
And many of the same sect will be killed.

The year 1666. The year of the Great Fire of London was foretold exactly in prose by the prophet as a divine retribution for the execution of Charles I. The "ancient lady" is said to reflect the dome of St. Paul's Cathedral, which collapsed from the blazing heat. It fell down on the heads of hundreds who sought shelter from the firestorm inside the massive building.

C9Q7:
The man who opens the tomb when it is found
And who does not close it immediately,
Evil will come to him
That no one will be able to prove.

The year 1791. This is a favorite quatrain among Nostradamus translators. They often quote it as validation of the prophets' power in that he foretold his own death. The legend goes that one night during the French Revolution, a group of drunken soldiers broke into the tomb where Nostradamus had been laid to rest in 1566. One soldier tore open the casket and scattered the bones. Believing the current rumor that the one who drinks from the skull of Nostradamus will have the powers of the prophet, another poured wine in the skull and drank. However, before the drunken soldier could swallow a sip, a shot rang out from the dark. The bullet pierced his heart, and he died instantly. His murderer was never found. Experts on Nostradamus insist that the prophecy was fulfilled.

C1Q60:
An emperor will be born near Italy.
He will cost his empire dearly; they will say that from the sort of people who surround him that he is less a prince than a butcher.

August 15, 1769. This quatrain is translated to mean the birth of Napoleon Bonaparte, born near Corsica, and the first of Nostradamus's three Antichrists.

C3Q35:
From the deepest part of Western Europe,
A young child will be born to poor people:
Who by his speech will seduce a great multitude,
His reputation will increase in the Kingdom of the East.

The year 1889. This quatrain has been translated to indicate the birth of Adolf Hitler, Nostradamus's second Antichrist and the man responsible for more than 50 million deaths during the six years of World War II.

C2Q10:
Before long everything will be organized
We await a very evil century:
The lot of the masked and solitary ones [clergy] greatly changed,
Few will be found who wish to stay in their places.

Nostradamus is believed to have foretold the details of the twentieth century with this quatrain and others. From his words, he apparently thought that this would be an evil and dangerous time. Many people believe that's not far from the truth. Like the visions of John in the Book of Revelation, Nostradamus believed that citizens of the world would be numbered, recorded, categorized and organized. With the vast computerized networks available today, along with social security numbers and various credit-checking systems, this prediction alone may be enough for some of his supporters to validate all of Nostradamus's predictions.

C6Q37:
The ancient work will be accomplished,
And from the roof evil ruin will fall on the great man.
Being dead they accuse an innocent of the deed:
the guilty one is hidden in the misty woods.

Noon, November 22, 1963. If the above predictions aren't enough to convince students of the prophet's accuracy, this one often does. It supposedly refers directly to the assassination of President John F. Kennedy, in Dallas, Texas. Those who have translated Nostradamus say the prophet was right down to the details, including "from the roof evil ruin will fall on the great man," referring to the shot that came from the roof of the book depository and struck Kennedy as he was riding in an open car. Additionally, the phrase, "being dead they accuse an innocent of the deed," seems to concur with reports that there were two shots fired and that Oswald may not have been in the right position to have killed the president. The final phrase—"the guilty one is hidden in the misty woods"—seems to suggest that one of the shots came from a grove of trees, where the gunman was obscured from the crowd's view.

Supposedly, Nostradamus talks about the disaster of Chernobyl, the Yom Kippur War (which he refers to as the beginning of World War III) and the AIDS epidemic, as reflected in C9Q55:

C9Q55:
A horrible war which is being prepared in the West,
The following year the pestilence will come,

So very horrible that young nor old,
nor animal [may survive].
Blood, fire, Mercury, mars, Jupiter in France.

The final line is said to have indicated September 1993.

IN C3Q75, HE WROTE:
Swords damp with blood from distant lands. A very great plague will
come with a great scab. Relief near but the remedies far away.

Nostradamus's translators say that the "swords damp with
blood from distant lands" is a direct reference to AIDS, with
"swords" referring to the disease's transmission through sexual
penetration, and "blood from distant lands" reflecting the fact that
the plague had started abroad. The sentence "Relief near but the
remedies far away," is taken to mean that while the victims are
made comfortable and medicine has been found to prolong life, the
cure has yet to be found.

Before the spread of AIDS, the two quatrains were said by
champions of Nostradamus's predictions to have foretold the
Spanish flu epidemic of 1918, which killed thousands and was
considered to be the worst plague of modern times.

In a letter from Nostradamus to King Henry II regarding his
psychic predictions, the prophet confides that the twentieth century
will view the greatest plague ever to be experienced. The disease will
make a dangerous time even more ominous. A translated version
reads as follows:

> . . .Then the impurities and abominations will be brought to
> the surface and made manifest. . .towards the end of a
> change in reign [thought to be the ending of Queen
> Elizabeth's reign].
> "The leaders of the Church will be backward in their
> love of God. . .Of the three sects, the Catholic is thrown into
> decadence by the partisan differences of its worshippers. The

Protestants will be entirely undone in all of Europe and part of Africa by the Islamics, by means of poor in spirit who, by madmen an antichrist or terrorists shall through world luxury [possibly oil] commit adultery...in the mean time [there appears to be] a plague that thirds of the world will fall and decay. So many die that no one will know the true owners of fields and houses. The weeds in the city streets will rise higher than the knees, and there shall be a total desolation of the Clergy.

Nostradamus's critics declare that the interpretations as well as the original text of his tangled prose are far too loose to be verified, considered valuable or reliable. His critics discount or fail to mention Nostradamus's use of proper names, such as Louis Pasteur. Some metaphysical scholars insist only fools would disparage Nostradamus's predictions. They point out that he was correct more than half of the time. The reason he doesn't have a better batting average is that we simply do not yet understand the allusions of the language he used. This information must come from the future, if the future allows us to see it unfold.

"Nostradamus always believed that it is possible to alter the predicted course of the future through awareness and action," writes Rosemary Ellen Guiley, author of *Harper's Encyclopedia of Mystical and Paranormal Experience*. "If his prophecies have been interpreted accurately in terms of the wars and disasters that have come to pass, humankind has made precious little headway toward mastering its fate."

DOOMSDAY'S GLUT

In mainstream religious and academic circles, there have been more than three thousand books and studies of millennial movements and forecasts. Some have been commentaries on the times in which we live as well as reflections on ancient prophecies. Some of the books and studies have been written to prepare sect followers to withstand current pressures and prepare for the new order, the Second Coming and/or Armageddon. This, according to some historians, was the case with the Book of Revelation.

Even the true believers of the End take offense at being grouped together with "the others." They often become indignant about the millenarian label. It is curious, however, that the more enthusiastic or revolutionary doomsayers are in their opinions, the more insistent they are that their concepts for a new world are neither illusory nor doomed.

Millennium movements generally have been known in two basic versions: Premillennial theology holds that Jesus will return before the millennium in order to establish a kingdom on earth. The postmillennialists teach that Christ will return after the millennial kingdom has already been established by humanity, the preaching of the gospel and the work of the church. The Puritans and the Pilgrims were overwhelmingly premillennial in the early days of the American colonies. They left England in a state of chaos; times were appalling, worse than anyone could ever remember. There was death, famine and dreadful storms. The scope of poverty was beyond belief. They were joyful that it was the End but afraid too. Many God-fearing folks knew the End was forthcoming. Why else would times be so tough? The pilgrim groups and other settlers in the Americas had a mission.

Like other religious radicals, they took chances. They sailed a nearly uncharted Atlantic and set up settlements *from scratch* in order to build a new society, one where they could dedicate themselves to God until He came. The New World represented the promised land. Other premillennialists, from Jim Jones to David Koresh and his Branch Davidians, have led their followers to a place that is sanctioned by their religious faith, where they either leave the terror of the final days behind or prepare for the final days by stockpiling food and ammunition. Many groups make enormous sacrifices in doing so.

With time, they became postmillennialists, believing that they must spread Christianity before Christ would come. Religion became the basis of "In God We Trust" and the backbone of America, democracy and consumerism. Those ethics are still with us today.

In chapter 4, we'll look at the spread of religion and spirituality in the United States. As the country began to notice that the second millennium was approaching, new sects and faiths sprang up. Some were hotly apocalyptic and some of them are still with us today, preaching the End.

Be warned, before you flip the page, that you may find yourself wanting to prepare for the End as you read on. And, Doomsayers tell us, the clock is still ticking and the hands are moving toward the end.

We are at the beginning of the second week.
We are children of the eighth day.

—Thornton Wilder, playwright

4

OLD TIME RELIGION FINDS A NEW SPIRIT

*R*evival meetings. Séances. Spirit-filled prophets. In post-Revolutionary War America, people were suddenly fascinated with the future—and a spirited future it was sure to be.

The resurgence of spirituality and religion in the United States from post-Revolutionary War times to the early 1920s can be compared to the surge of Fundamentalism we've experienced in the past 10 years. The revivals seem to come in cycles, and by 1820 there was a rekindling of that old-time religion the likes of which this country had never seen. There were Presbyterians, the Methodists and the Baptists. The fire-and-brimstone preachers of each sect pleaded with sinners to confess and repent, thus avoiding the devil pits offered by the other two sects.

59

In this chapter, we'll take a look at the people and events that captivated the American public and how they have shaped spirituality in this country. In this spiritual rebirth, sometimes referred to as the "heyday of Spiritualism," mediums, psychics, fortunetellers, mystics, magicians and hustlers of the mystical realm became a hot commodity. Séances became a pop phenomenon and in parlors throughout the country, people talked about contacting long-dead loved ones and communicating with those on the "other side." The thirst for occult knowledge seemed impossible to satisfy.

During this period—1770 to the early 1900s—attendance in secret societies soared as interest in ceremonial magic, ancient alchemy and psychic powers returned. Memberships mushroomed in groups that believed they were living on the Eve of Destruction.

The country was suffering. Inflation and poverty touched almost every household—including the home of our country's first president—after the Revolutionary War. Then came other conflicts: The War of 1812, the Civil War, the Spanish-American War and hundreds of unnamed confrontations between U.S. soldiers and Native Americans. Because strife brings about a quest to understand "why," people began to return to God for their answers. Therefore, not only was there a resurgence of interest in the occult, but thousands returned to the old-time religions.

Ann Lee (1736-1784), once a member of the Quakers or Society of Friends in England, moved to America, proclaiming that she was the reincarnation of Christ. The group advocated shared possessions and sexual equality and gave religion a new twist by including dancing and singing in the services. She preached celibacy, godliness, cleanliness and devotion and founded the Shaker communities in America. "Mother" Lee claimed to have received a revelation that the maternal element of Christ's spirit was resurrected in her. The world did not end when she died, nor did her following splinter. Shaker communities were established, but since the group preached celibacy, their numbers dwindled.

Other religious gurus and self-appointed Christs appeared after the American Revolution. Isaac Bullard, dressed in a bearskin girdle, led his devotees out of the madness of modern society and championed free love along with a primitive form of communism. He believed he was the "Anointed One" mentioned in the Bible. (Bullard also believed it was a sin to wash and supposedly wore the same clothing throughout his adult life.)

Jemima Wilkinson believed herself to be Christ. Believers flocked to her, and she led them through divine revelation (what today we might describe as channeled information from a spiritual source). Abel Sargent also talked with angels. He preached the message that he was Christ in New York State in 1812. With 12 women as his apostles, he claimed he could raise the dead and that he never needed to eat, since he was immortal.

One of the most intriguing religious revolutions started with a poor but honest farmer. The movement swept the entire country, and its offshoots, including the Seventh-Day Adventists and the Jehovah's Witnesses, are still gathering hundreds of thousands of followers today. Say hello to William Miller, the quiet man from New England who revolutionized our country's thoughts on Doomsday.

"MAD MILLER" AND THE END

William Miller was an impoverished Massachusetts farmer who lived from 1782-1849 and struggled to make a living on a rocky chunk of land. He was so distraught after he returned from military service in the War of 1812 that he turned his energy from the soil to seek answers in Christianity. He had returned home from the army shaken by the brutality, the carnage, the suffering, the senseless death, the mass destruction of humanity and the innocents destroyed by war.

Before the war, William Miller had been a confirmed atheist. Afterward, he could find no respite until he put his life in the hands of God, via a Baptist revival service. At age 34, he was converted and began fervently to seek Christ and pray for His Second Coming. Shortly thereafter, Miller became a licensed preacher with a small, thoughtful following. During his diligent study of the Scriptures, he realized that Christ was about to return, not someday in the far reaches of the future but in the next few years. With careful consideration and in full awareness of the consequences, he announced to his congregation that he knew *exactly* when Christ would return. Like wildfire, word spread, and many prepared for the final judgment.

Miller came to the notice of a great number of New Englanders when he began to publicly divine the Second Coming of Christ. Although he was still the same quiet backwoods preacher, he began to amass a large following as he zeroed in on specific dates for the event. End Times groupies followed him wherever he went. Questioning Christians joined his cause. Those who had no previous religious inclination became believers.

Without Miller's participation or even his knowledge, groups formed and selected leaders to preach the End as Miller did. In 1839, when Miller met then-converted Joshua V. Himes, the movement changed from a one-man show to a religious extravaganza. "Miller fever" looked like it might sweep the nation with Miller at its center.

When established faiths began losing members, a few ministers became hostile and spread lies that Miller was a deranged lunatic, a menacing fraud bent on deceiving the youth of the country and/or a cult fanatic. There were reports that Miller mesmerized those who attended the revival meetings.

The prophet became known as "Mad Miller" in the press. Protestant and Catholic groups condemned him and his teachings as modern-day heresy, warning their faithful that to follow Miller would mean hell and damnation forever.

Nevertheless, Miller's End Time predictions caught the imagination of religious extremists and enthusiasts, and the watchers of the movement became participants. In the beginning, Miller refused to divulge a specific date for the end, although insiders knew it. Instead he proclaimed that the End would occur "about the year 1843."

In the January 4, 1843 edition of *Signs of the Times*, the Millerite publication, he flatly denied the widely acclaimed idea that the End was to be in April, possibly April 23. The article said, "The fact is that the believers of the second advent in 1843 *have fixed* NO TIME *in the year* for the event. And Brethren Miller, Himes, Litch, Hale, Fitch, Hawley, and other prominent lecturers, most decidedly protest against. . .giving the day or hour of the event. This we have done over and over again, in our paper." Another article says, "It is true that individual preachers or limited groups here and there sought to find a Scriptural analogy or by a certain reading of the prophecy a warrant for predicting the advent on some particular day during the year."

Even with the denials that came from the Miller camp, the movement barely took a breath. More so, the heavens seemed to confirm the coming of the Apocalypse with a great meteor show as a comet flashed across the sky. The star show appeared to corroborate the prophecy of the End in the Bible that says with "signs and wonders" Christ will come. The prophecy was substantiated. (In the same years that Miller was preaching his doctrine of the End, other deviant Christian groups, including the Mormons, were gaining attention. The Shaker movement grew, and communal Christian groups such as the Ebenezer Society and the Bethel Community also attracted public interest.)

Miller wasn't alone in believing that times couldn't get much worse. There were terrible moral struggles occurring in the United States over such issues as slavery, states' rights, taxes, inflation, human rights, the vote for women, poverty and increased crime and incurable diseases. Many people were more than ready to believe that they were living in the time of the Tribulation. Not only did people leave their churches to join Miller's group and others, but some even changed their entire lifestyle disposing of property, ceasing to plant crops and giving their savings to the poor and to the Millerite movement. Like the Montanists long before, they would need nothing when Jesus Christ came and didn't want to be burdened with possessions. They declared themselves ready to meet their Maker. They were devoted to the End.

On January 1, 1943, William Miller published a synopsis of his beliefs:

> I believe the time can be known by all who desire to understand and to be ready for His coming. And I am fully convinced that sometime between March 21st, 1843 and March 21st, 1844, according to the Jewish mode of computation of time, Christ will come, and bring all His Saints with Him; and that then He will reward every man as his work shall be.

The fervor continued and the Miller message spread through word of mouth, the revivals and publications produced by the Millerite movement, including the *Philadelphia Alarm*, the *Signs of the Times* and the *Midnight Cry*. Newspapers picked up the story. End Times propaganda was published and distributed by the Millerite leaders in various cities, especially in connection with upcoming lectures or revival meetings.

It wasn't only the established churches which ridiculed, condemned, feared and fought to stop Miller and the Millerites. Many people had doubts. Many voiced disbelief that the End could be forecast by a simple backwoods preacher from New England and many believed that Miller was crazy and a threat to society. Supporters of Miller pointed out that Jesus was the target of similar accusations.

In spite of growing opposition, the Millerite movement gained momentum. In some cities and towns it became impossible to find a hall large enough to hold their meetings; their numbers were growing that fast. And in 1843, the leaders decided to build a tabernacle in Boston. It was dedicated with great pomp and circumstance in front of a group of more than three thousand followers. "The Millerites have very properly been shut out of the buildings in which they have for some time been holding their orgies in Philadelphia," wrote a newspaper reporter in 1843, "and we are happy to learn that the grand jury of the Boston municipal court has represented the great temple itself as a dangerous structure. After some half-dozen more deaths occur and a few more men and women are sent to madhouses by this miserable fanaticism perhaps some grand jury may think it worthwhile to indict the vagabonds who are the cause of so much mischief."

When April 23 came and went without a hint of the return of Jesus Christ or the cataclysmic terrors that were expected, a few of the followers dropped out and walked away, but most of the Millerites become even more enthusiastic. After all, there was a whole year in which to look for the Second Coming. At the end of 1843, the Second Coming still hadn't transpired, but Miller and his followers were surprisingly undismayed. In a New Year's address to his congregation, Miller said:

"Brethren: The Roman [year] 1843 is past [the Jewish sacred year would end in the spring of 1844] and our hopes are not realized. Shall we give up the ship? No, no. . .We do not believe our reckoning has run out. It takes all of 457 and 1843 to make 2300, and must of course run as far into '44 as it began in the year 457 before Christ."

At this time, according to the historian C. E. Sears, there was a fluttering of doubt and a tingling of hesitation on the part of certain communities of Millerites. "[S]oon those were dispelled when it was recalled that as far back as 1839 Prophet Miller had stated on some occasion which had been forgotten in the general excitement, that he was not *positive* that the event would take place during the *Christian* year from 1843 to 1844, and that he would claim the whole *Jewish* year which would carry the prophecy over to the 21st of March, 1844. An announcement to this effect was made, and by this time the delusion had taken such a firm hold upon the imaginations of his followers that any simple explanation, however crude, seemed sufficient to quiet all doubts and questions."

The brethren accepted this revision and renewed their work with vigor. Sears explains that the Millerites seemed to be driven to terrify the army of unbelievers "into the realization of the horrors that awaited them to strengthen the faith of those already in his ranks." These tactics worked for the number of followers grew.

When the original Doomsday date passed without event, the press and public had a field day. The world made merry over the Prophet Miller's predicament and the taunts and jeers of the scoffers were nearly unbearable. Miller's followers were subjected to merciless ridicule wherever they went. One Boston newspaper ran the headline "What!—not gone up yet?—We thought you'd gone up! Aren't you going up soon?—Wife didn't go up and leave you behind to burn, did she?" Journalists and politicians, doctors and town drunks—everyone in every community, it seemed, refused to leave the issue alone.

Then came the end of the year in the year that the world should have ended. But the End didn't come. Once more, even though some devotees fell from the fold, the overall intensity and zeal didn't slow but became even stronger. This failure seemed to ignite followers who had so long prayed for salvation. And by the end of July, 1844, thousands more were being converted to Millerism, which followers took as one more fulfillment of the Bible's End Times prophecies.

It was during the summer of '44 that the brethren of the Millerites came out with the *real* day, a new day for the End;

October 22, 1844. The *Midnight Cry* and other Millerite publications went into overtime, cranking out tons of End Times literature. Followers preached the End and preachers preached the End. Those who had never before considered the matter wondered if it could be the End. Ministers of the established churches were wondering if they should worry too—and if they had time. End Times fever had truly caught hold. Miller mania swept an entire country.

The *Midnight Cry* reported that many people were leaving their jobs and homes to warn the population about the end of the world. "In Philadelphia, thirteen volunteered at one meeting (after hearing Brother Storrs) to go out and sound the alarm. . .In both cities [New York and Philadelphia], stores are being closed, and they preach in tones the world understands, though they may not heed it."

Paul Kurtz, a philosopher, humanist, founding chairman of the Committee for the Scientific Investigation of Claims of the Paranormal, and author of *Transcendental Temptation*, explains that Miller had an interesting sideline going as the End approached and that he "reaped a considerable sum of money by selling his followers white ascension robes." When his actions were challenged by established church groups, Miller countered that he was simply doing God's work. He "knew" that Jesus Christ wanted Christians to be appropriately dressed and the robes were the proper attire in which to meet Jesus Christ on His return.

While Miller didn't promote any specific area from which to view Christ's coming, many people got the idea that the higher up one was, the better was the chance to be the first to witness Jesus Christ's arrival. (New Age doomsayers believe that the entire world will "see" the event through a conscious connection that will unite all of humanity. It will be, they say, as if each of us had a little satellite dish of the event in our heads. They believe after the great disruption of world services, we surely will not see it on the six o'clock news.)

In the collected recollections of Clara Endicott Sears, whose book *Days of Delusion* was published in 1924, the author writes:

One man (I will not use names, as his descendants might not like) put on turkey wings, got up in a tree and prayed that the Lord would take him up. He tried to fly, fell and broke his arm. . .I remember well my father and mother talking about it. I remember hearing them say that some went insane over it.

David Cohen in *Waiting for the Apocalypse*, recounts Sears's memories and reiterates that, anecdotal or not, some disillusioned Millerites were committed to state asylums. Several committed murder or suicide.

On March 21, 1844, a Boston journalist who was following the story, reported to the *New York Herald* that many Millerites jumped from the bluffs and treetops in the belief that with Christ's return, they'd be able to defy the law of gravity. Unfortunately for the zealots, Newton's law of gravity prevailed that day, and Jesus Christ did not return. Those who jumped were critically hurt, and some fell to their deaths. People were grief-stricken, and Miller confessed his mistake, showing both shock and acute embarrassment. Yet he attempted to convince the dwindling congregation the End would come. Really it would.

When the second D day, October 22, 1844, didn't arrive as predicted, Miller and his followers were severely frustrated. They had worn the special robes, had gone out to the countryside to convert the masses and had preached the End Times gospel. They had climbed trees, hiked up mountainsides and crawled to the tops of barns waiting, praying, believing and watching for the Savior to come. Their devotion to the Second Coming was that strong. This final lack of confirmation is known as the Great Disappointment.

Miller had explained his initial failures at date-setting as the result of a stall in Doomsday, or a "tarrying time," referred to in Habakkuk 2:3. This time that theory didn't set right with his followers.

Though one might suppose it would take only a single instance of disillusion to collapse an End Times sect, it often takes many. With the Millerites there were three, perhaps four. The last one was too much even for the zealous leaders, and they fell to dissension, quarreling and public humiliation. By the spring of 1845, the group had practically disappeared, and Miller withdrew from public scrutiny.

Those who continued to believe at least a portion of what Miller had to say were disputing such things as whether the soul sleeps from the hour of death until Judgment Day or not, and if the sabbath should be celebrated on Saturday or Sunday, and whether the rite of baptism should be administered through sprinkling or total immersion. Additionally, there was debate as to whether anyone should or could set the date for Christ's return. They'd seen what it had done to Miller and some had experienced the ridicule firsthand when the Disappointment came.

Nevertheless, Miller has had an extraordinary influence on American evangelical movements, including the Jehovah's Witnesses and the Seventh-Day Adventists. Although much of his reasoning has been accused of being speculative, much of it is based on the Bible as the literal word of God, especially focusing on the Book of Daniel in the Old Testament and the Book of Revelation in the New Testament, which foretell the Last Days, Armageddon and the Second Coming. The force of the Millerite Movement didn't really die. Miller, however, never had the opportunity to receive joy from the influence of his movement. Four years after the Great Disappointment, bitter with frustration, Miller died, cheated of experiencing the Second Coming he had predicted for years.

Miller's followers reorganized into four main Fundamentalist groups, which still continue to flourish. A shift of members from the more liberal to the more Evangelical denominations is evidence that folks are seeking to heed a more intense kind of faith than their current church provides. Social scientists call the new groups sects.

There have been hundreds of new sects formed during American history as dissidents broke away, believing that their former group had lost sight of specific values or ideals. The Pilgrims, Puritans, Quakers and Shakers all began as splinter groups. The dissidents have, according to sociologists, usually been strong in their convictions as they break away and return to the fundamentals of their faith. As denominations grow and prosper they often dilute their intensity on the Scriptures in an attempt to embrace more followers.

One of the Miller splinter groups still with us today and still praying for the End was founded by Ellen B. White (1827-1915) and her husband, James, and Joseph Bates. Together, they officially formed the Seventh-Day Adventists in 1863. Two tenets of Fundamentalism are still adhered to by the group: (1) belief in the visible personal Second Coming of Christ at an early but indefinite date, and (2) celebration of Saturday as the Sabbath. As with other Fundamentalist groups, Seventh-Day Adventists accept the Bible as the only religious authority and believe that they receive special guidance through the literal interpretation of the prophetic passages. Adventists still recognize the Great Disappointment as part of their history.

Other offshoots of the Millerite movement include the Church of God, the Advent Christian Church and the Primitive Advent Church. These groups maintain that the End is nigh, that terrible times are upon us, that Jesus Christ will return and that the return of Christ will precede the millennial kingdom of God as predicted in Revelation 20:1-6.

WATCHING FOR THE END

One of the most significant Millerite splinter groups was formed by Charles Taze Russell (1852-1916). Russell was influenced early on by the philosophical remnant of the Millerite movement, although there is no evidence that Russell ever personally met William Miller.

In about 1870, Russell visited a group called the Second Advent. This Christian-based Fundamentalist organization, taking some ideas from Miller, predicted that the End would occur between 1873 and 1874—only, of course, to be disappointed. The Millerite foundations of searching the Bible for prophecy and instruction and the belief that Jesus Christ would return so influenced Russell that they combined to form the cornerstone of the Jehovah's Witnesses (officially known as the Watchtower Bible and Tract Society). Since 1881, it has been one of the most loyal and outspoken of the Doomsday Fundamentalist groups.

Russell's Jehovah's Witnesses have been promising the End was in sight since the group was first organized in 1884, and have set dates a number of times, too. The Second Coming is at the heart of the religious movement. At least five times in this century the Watchtower Bible and Tract Society has predicted the End (the most recent date was 1975). *The Time Is at Hand*, a volume of Witness doctrine published in 1908, states:

> We consider it an established truth that the final end of the kingdoms of this world, and the full establishment of the Kingdom of God will be accomplished at the end of A.D. 1914.

When 1914 came and went, founder Charles Taze Russell informed his followers that in fact Christ, in the form of the Archangel Michael, had defeated Satan and established his kingdom in the outer heavens. Russell said that the public had misunderstood. The prediction hadn't meant that Christ would take up the throne on earth.

During the period from 1914 to 1918, Russell prophesied that "millions living now will never die." The War of Armageddon and the dawning of the millennium were supposed to occur before the last of the 144,000 specially appointed followers died. Critics point out however that by 1984, only about 10,000 of those 144,000 were in fact living and breathing; the rest had passed on.

Yet, the End Times predictions continued. Once more, the date was moved forward, to 1918. Once more, the End didn't come. This time, followers didn't receive a retraction or an apology. Instead, they were told that another important celestial event had occurred. According to the church's governing body, Christ came into God's temple in order to cleanse it. Thus, human followers were unable to know of the incident except through the word of church leaders.

Church leaders continued to forecast Doomsday again in 1920, then 1925 and then 1941. Then 1975 was said to *really* be it, this time. How did they come to the conclusion that it would be 1975? According to the dogma and the society's arithmetic system, Adam's creation happened in 4026 B.C., thus in the Witnesses' view six thousand years of human history as we know it would come to an abrupt halt in 1975. When that date passed, thousands left the sect, dismayed and disillusioned. Those who protested were often openly shunned by others in the congregation. (In the Jehovah's Witnesses sect, when an individual has been disfellowshipped from the society, he or she is avoided. Witnesses also have been known to shun members of their own families, even those who live in the same home, for not following the tenets of the strict doctrine.)

Yet the exuberance of the remaining members, each of whom is required to work 15 to 50 hours a week to preach their gospel, has resulted in growing numbers of new recruits. The society's publication, *The Watchtower*, has a circulation of over twelve million; *Awake* is distributed to over eight million. More than one billion Bibles, books and booklets have been distributed by the sect since 1920.

Another prediction concerning the End may be needed shortly. With no specific date cited, the current prophecy for

Doomsday is to be within the early years of the next century. Some young Witnesses are ready and waiting for the Supreme Ruler to guide the earth after Armageddon. Interestingly, before he changed his religious views, the singer Michael Jackson was the society's most famous member, and many younger Witnesses believed for a time he was the Messiah. Older, more conservative members were shocked and denied that Jackson was the One. Now, most members are continuing to wait for the society's governing body to tell them once more the when and how of Doomsday.

THE PROPHET JOSEPH SMITH

At the same time that William Miller was proclaiming the End, what has now become the largest and most successful Christian denomination in the United States was being born. The Mormon church, or, as it is officially known, the Church of Jesus Christ of Latter Day Saints, was being founded by Joseph Smith, Jr. (1805-1844). Although the prophets never met, they had much in common since they were both zealously preparing for the End.

Conceived in controversy and steeped in doctrine, the Mormons have been prosecuted for their End Times beliefs. Smith, according to scholars such as Paul Kurtz, author of *The Transcendental Temptation*, started his career as a necromancer (one who spiritually contacts the dead and is usually paid for the service), a glass looker and a treasure hunter. His father attempted to eke out a living as a dowser. Kurtz writes that Joseph Jr. "maintained that he could see things by looking into the stone. Interestingly, Joseph Smith was indicted and tried in 1826, at the age of twenty-one, for being a 'disorderly person and an imposter.'" Smith was convicted on his own testimony that he used spells, magical arts and incantations to produce desired results. It seems that his clients were unhappy that he was unable to find gold or other treasures using these methods. This was only the beginning of the storm of controversy that would surround Smith and the Mormons (the name is derived from Mormon, father to the angel Moroni).

Smith received his spiritual revelation on the nights of September 21 and 22, 1823, when his room was filled with a brilliant white light revealing the angel Moroni. Moroni brought a message from God telling Smith that he was descended from an ancient people of Israel who had emigrated to the Americas. Smith was told that Christ had appeared to the American tribe after the resurrection. Christ established a church, but the gospel had been lost in a war. God had appointed Smith to retrieve the buried plates, translate the Scriptures through the use of "seer stones" and resurrect the church. He was also to prepare himself, his family and his followers for the Latter Days.

Much has been written about the tumultuous struggle of Smith and his new followers as they attempted to populate the world with Mormons (since Mormons were the chosen people). Many, including Smith, died for defending their religious beliefs or as bystanders for their cause, but the religion didn't perish. Eventually the movement spread to Utah, where the first of many great temples was erected.

The Mormons believe that there will be three great events before the end of the world. First, they must regroup from all over the globe to Independence, Missouri, which they believe to be the modern-day Zion. Second, the Jews must gather in Palestine because when Jesus returns, He will reside in both Palestine and Independence. Third, there will be a regathering of the 10 lost tribes spoken of in the Bible, and they will assemble in Zion.

During the millennium, according to the Mormons, two resurrections will be conducted. When Christ descends to the earth from the heavens, they believe that the righteous will be resurrected to meet the Lord and then descend back with Him. This is in contrast to the evangelical belief that the righteous will be transported directly to heaven. At the beginning of Jesus Christ's reign on earth, the wicked will be destroyed by fire. The spirits of these dead will reside in hell or in a special prison house, where they will continue to suffer for sins as a form of atonement. Then will come the peaceful millennium. At this time, Mormons will conduct baptism for the dead, led by Christ, in order that those who were not brought into the fold during their lifetime may enter it after death.

At the end of this peaceful period, there will be a second resurrection, during which the wicked shall be raised. Satan will be released from his prison, and the forces of evil will unite in a war against Jesus Christ. He will defeat evil and make way for the Final Judgment.

The Final Judgment, according to the Mormon beliefs, includes the real End, that is, the dissolution of the earth in preparation for eternity. The earth will be resurrected as a celestial body, much like the sun and stars of the universe. It will be on designated planets that the spirits of the Mormons, the non-Mormons and the really wicked will continue to exist. Mormons believe that when the End comes for humanity, they will achieve godhood on another planet (or on what was once earth but has been transformed into a better planet).

Mormons believe that God is eternal and the eternity of God means a prehuman spiritual existence for all humans, followed by a time of probation with a physical body. Then the spirit and body are evolved into the status of a godhood once again. Thus, Mormons cherish the idea that all of humanity is destined to become a god—if they are baptized Mormons. Lorenzo Snow, the fifth president of the Mormon church said, "As man is, God once was; as God is, man may become."

Rather than splinter and die when the leader's End Times prophecies were not fulfilled immediately, the Mormon church has been transformed from a "radical" cult that was persecuted by religious mobs and the government and the established churches of the day into a defender of family values and moral righteousness. Today, Kurtz and other religious experts explain, the Mormons are regarded as industrious and highly ethical people and are extremely patriotic. Was Joseph Smith a divine prophet? Or a clever imposter? The life and works of the founder have been well-researched and documented, yet in order to make a judgment one must take sides on the question of whether or not this is the End.

THE SLEEPING PROPHET PREDICTS THE END

While some Americans of the late 1800s were returning to their religious convictions or accepting revolutionary End Times theories such as those of Joseph Smith and Charles Taze Russell, others were delving into the supernatural (although that term wasn't coined until much later). According to teachers, thinkers and students of the occult, theories regarding the End ran the gamut from a total transformation of the universe, by God or some other power, to seismic catastrophes that would transfigure the face of the earth, killing millions of people. Even in the late nineteenth century, one of the most popular occult End Times theories was that massive earthquakes would transform the planet.

American psychic Edgar Cayce (1877-1945) had a lot to do with directing that thought. He also had a lot to say about the limited future of our planet.

During deep psychic trances, Cayce would channel spiritual energies that would predict, among other things, events affecting our world. (The trances were so deep that he was often referred to as the "sleeping prophet.") Some New Agers cite the Bible, in particular Numbers 12:6, to support their view that Cayce's arrival was preordained. The Scripture reads: "If there be a prophet among you, I the Lord will make myself known unto him in a vision, and will speak unto him in a dream." (Other messiahs and prophets have named this same Scripture as evidence that they are the One.)

Cayce predicted the End a number of times, and his words, channeled from a spiritual realm, are recorded in massive texts still referred to by students, scholars and researchers. A caring, devoted family man, Cayce was not a physician or a geologist, but his psychic medical advice was normally 90 percent correct, and scientists have discovered that his geological predictions were also amazingly accurate.

Many of Cayce's predictions, according to followers, have already been realized, from food shortages and overpopulation to earthquakes and devastating wars. Cayce believed that human action could alter fate, and failure to change a course of action could result in disaster.

Cayce taught that near the end of this century there would be tremendous geographic changes in the planet. He believed that earthquakes would cause the Great Lakes to drain, turning the entire Midwest into one great ocean where the Mississippi Valley is now. He saw great masses of land being lost to water and the breadbasket of America drowning in floods. There would be sweeping food shortages within the United States, and since the United States is the main supplier of grain and provisions, the entire world could eventually starve. Cayce said, "Saskatchewan, the Pampas areas of the Argentine . . . portions of South Africa . . . these rich areas, with some portion of Montana and Nevada, must feed the world!"

But not all will be underwater. Cayce predicted that new land will appear in the Atlantic Ocean when the End comes. Among the land masses to spring forth will be a new continent called Poseidon, which he believed was the mythical Atlantis. Regardless of what one thinks of this concept, in 1974 geologists discovered what they believe to be part of Atlantis off the Bimini Islands in the Bahamas, exactly where Cayce had predicted the new land mass would eventually rise.

In a channeling session in 1932, Cayce was asked how soon the changes in the earth would begin and what signs should we look for as signals to the End of the world as we know it. Cayce replied from his trance, "When there is the first breaking up of some conditions of the South Seas [the South Pacific] and sinking or rising in the Mediterranean, and the Etna area, then we know it has begun." This area of Etna in the South Pacific, according to geologists, is the western boundary of the Pacific plate, the most seismically active area of the world. It is extremely unlikely that Cayce, who was only educated through high school, could have known this. Yet he predicted the world would quake and that new land areas would appear, and New Age followers of the prophet point out that this has already begun to occur. In 1977, in the Solomon Islands of the South Pacific, there were four massive quakes that ranged from 7.2 to 8.1 on the Richter scale, and they spouted up a temporary land area. In 1978 and 1979, three submarine eruptions of volcanos produced more new land, some beneath the ocean and some a bit above. In fact, the South Pacific has received over 11 percent of all seismic activity recorded in the world in the past 20 years.

Cayce didn't stop with forecasting changes in the South Seas, Atlantic Ocean and Great Lakes. He also foretold, as a signal of the End, that a great portion of Japan (where the Pacific and Eurasian plates are jammed together) would tumble into the sea and that the upper portion of Europe would "change as in a twinkling of an eye."

In 1941, Cayce foresaw that the great battlefields of the world would "become oceans, bays and lands over which the new order will carry on their trade one with another." This was seen as continents breaking apart and new portions of lands appearing. Cayce predicted, "There will be open water appearing in the northern portions of Greenland, and South America will be shaken up from the uppermost portion to the end." And of our country, Cayce said, "The greater change will be in the North Atlantic Seaboard. Watch New York, Connecticut and the like," Cayce admonished. "Many portions of the East Coast will be disturbed, as well as many portions of the West Coast, as well as the central portion of the United States. Los Angeles and San Francisco, most of all these will be among those that will be destroyed, before New York, even. Portions of the now East Coast of New York or New York City itself, will in the main disappear."

Regarding the "Big One" that Californians so often refer to, Cayce said that as the End approaches, there will be many land changes along the California coast. And "If there are the great activities in the Vesuvius, of Pelee [this may be a reference to the Island Pele, in the South Pacific, rather than Mount Pelee], then the south coast of California, and the areas between Salt Lake and the southern portions of Nevada—may expect within the three months following same, an inundation by earthquakes. But these, as we find, are to be more in the Southern than in the Northern Hemisphere." While Cayce didn't specifically say that the San Andreas Fault would be the focal point of destruction, as popularly thought until the Los Angeles quake of 1994, he did believe that one of the signs of complete change in the world would be that much-laughed-at Arizona ocean property.

Cayce also divined that after the enormous changes brought about by seismic occurrences, we would see the earth's climate change. He said that the "extreme north portions [of the world] were then the southern portions—or the polar regions were then turned to where they occupied more of the tropical and semi-tropical regions. . . . There will be upheavals. . .that will make for the eruptions of volcanoes in the torrid areas, and there will be shifting then of the poles." This, according to Cayce's trance records, will occur about 2000-2001 A.D. Other New Agers believe that the Great Pyramid at Giza reflects that 2001 will coincide with Cayce's End Times report.

During one session concerning how the world would be changed after the upheavals, Cayce proceeded to discuss where there might be safe areas: Where could one survive the End? Cayce said, "Safety lands will be in the area around Norfolk and Virginia Beach, parts of Ohio, Indiana and Illinois and much of the southern portion of Canada and the vast portion of Canada." [Cayce's foundation, the Association for Research and Enlightenment (ARE) is located in Virginia Beach.] Although these areas have experienced earthquakes and thus are on fault lines, Cayce assured followers that the areas would be safe and one must expect the unexpected in the End Times. "Norfolk is to be a mighty good place, and a safe place when turmoil begins, though it may appear that it may be in the line of those areas to rise, while many higher land will sink. This is a good area to stick to."

Knowing of Cayce's D day scenario, thousands flocked to him for counsel on facing the coming years. Records indicate that he talked a great deal about this topic and gave many warnings to his followers. When asked, "What is needed most in the world today?," Cayce replied that humanity must be warned that "the day of the Lord is near at hand, and that those who have been and are unfaithful must meet themselves in those things which come to pass in their experience." When pressed by followers to expound on the meaning of "the day of the Lord," Cayce replied, "That as has been promised through the prophets and the sages of old, the time and a half time [this is a biblical reference to the time approaching the seven years of Tribulation] has been and is being fulfilled in this day and generation, and that soon there will again appear in the Earth that One through whom many will be called to meet those that are preparing the way for His day in the Earth. The

Lord then will come, even as ye have seen Him go." When pressed for a date, Cayce replied, "When those that are His have made the way clear, passable, for Him to come."

Is this, once more, Jesus's promise and revelation that the kingdom of God is within each of us? Some New Agers believe that when the End comes, there will be a complete change of consciousness rather than the terrible disasters foretold in the Bible's Book of Revelation. Cayce said that it is the activity of many, thinking positive thoughts, that "oft keep many a city and many a land intact," accomplished through the honoring of the spiritual laws.

The Sleeping Prophet also foretold of a change in the evolution of humanity after the End, should it come to pass as predicted. Telepathic powers, with the ability to psychically communicate with one another, will produce great social change and an improvement in the daily life of all people. Cayce said, "When there has been in the earth those groups that have sufficiently desired and sought peace, peace will begin. It must be within self."

It must be noted that from those who knew him and in his biographies, Edgar Cayce is remembered as a gentle, caring and religious individual. Although he discussed global devastation in broad detail, he wasn't numb to its implications. But Cayce was a staunch believer in reincarnation and therefore not overly concerned with the loss of life that would occur were the planet to shake, rattle and roll as prophesied. Cayce, like other advocates of reincarnation, believed that souls would be born again either as a human, animal or other life form, or perhaps move higher up into a spiritual form of existence.

Not all Christians agree with Cayce's ideas about reincarnation or with his prediction of the End. Bob Larson, author of *Larson's New Book of Cults*, accuses Cayce of giving false messages to Christians. "Even his proponents admit his prophecies have proven to be only 90 percent accurate," Larson wrote. "Critics place his rate of accuracy even lower." It is known that Cayce underestimated Hitler's diabolical impact on the world, and that he predicted New York City would fall into the Atlantic in the mid-seventies. Fundamentalists object to his belief in reincarnation and evolution (humanity descending from apes) and his occult methods, from astrology to astral projection. ARE encourages people to review its publications and Mary Ellen Carter's *My Years with Edgar Cayce* and to make their own decisions about the End Times prophecies.

Yet, if Cayce was on target even 90 percent of the time, or 50 percent of the time, his predictions stand a pretty good chance of hitting the D day bull's-eye.

ASLEEP BUT NOT ALONE

Doomsday prophets of the late 1800s and early 1900s traveled the country giving lectures on psychic odysseys. Most were paid to demonstrate their psychic skills.

Two people who have had a significant influence on New Age doomsayers are Madame Helena Petrovna Blavatsky (1831-1891) and Aleister Crowley (1875-1947). Blavatsky was a co-founder, with Henry Steel Olcott, of the Theosophy Society. Now often referred to as a New Age concept, Theosophy in fact began in New York in 1875 and became the basis for many contemporary metaphysical and religious splinter groups including the I AM movement. Crowley's leadership in the Hermetic Order of the Golden Dawn and other occult groups shaped the New Age movement we know today through a blend of alchemy, ESP and magical ceremony.

Informally known as HPB, Madame Blavatsky was a psychic of great talent, according to her own autobiography and other accounts of her life. The daughter of a Russian prince, HPB lived a bohemian life, a flower child long before anyone had heard the term. She traveled widely and had a charismatic personality.

Claiming that she received spiritual guidance from channeled energies, she was one of the first to provide a dogma that blended Eastern mystical practices (such as yoga and the use of chants) with Western thinking and religions. She caught the attention of the press and aroused American's curiosity about mysticism and forces beyond the known.

(For the record, contemporary Fundamentalists believe that Blavatsky, like other metaphysical and psychic cult leaders, was a Lucifer-loving heretic. They say that the Theosophy movement of the 1800s, like the New Age movement, is a lot of dangerous gibberish.)

Blavatsky was credited by many witnesses with incredible telepathic gifts. Supposedly, she had the ability to transport objects through the air, to receive messages from the dearly departed and connect with the spiritual energy of the universe. Later in her career, she was discredited by investigators from the Society for Psychical Research, an institute dedicated to investigating claims of the paranormal. According to the spiritual guidance she received from another realm, Madame Blavatsky predicted the end of our planet would occur in the year 2000. She believed we could change the course of fate, but only by becoming attuned with spiritual guidance.

Aleister Crowley believed that he himself was the long-prophesied Antichrist. Born on October 12, 1875, in Leamington Spa, Warwickshire, England, Crowley was reared by parents who were members of a strictly conservative sect. When he was a child, his mother nicknamed him "the beast," after the Antichrist. Like other teenagers he was rebellious, but his defiance took the form of a fascination with human blood, torture and sexual degradation.

Crowley so believed in reincarnation that he insisted that in past lives he had been Pope Alexander VI, Edward Kelly (the apprentice to Dr. John Dee, Queen Elizabeth I's astrologer) and the renowned ceremonial magician Eliphas Levi. Samuel

MacGregor Mathers, one of the founders of the secret society, the Hermetic Order of the Golden Dawn, initiated Crowley and taught him the sacred magic of Abra-Melin the Mage, a book of powerful spells and incantations. In the society, he studied magic, the occult and the ancient philosophy of Hebrew mysticism called the Kabbalah (many of the same things Nostradamus had learned). But Crowley wasn't satisfied with being a member of the sect, he tried to usurp the power of its leaders. When he failed, he embarked on his own. A British journalist wrote "Crowley is the wickedest man alive," and that sentiment pretty well summed up public opinion.

In 1904, Crowley and his wife, Rose, went to Cairo to study Egyptian occultism. During the trip, he and Rose performed magical rituals learned during his time with the Hermetic Order of the Golden Dawn. Suddenly Rose began to channel information regarding a statue of Horus, the Egyptian god, which was on exhibit at a nearby museum. The exhibit was number 666, the number of the Bible's Beast. Crowley was told through the spiritual energy of Horus that he was in fact the Great Beast foretold in the Book of Revelation, the Antichrist, and that he'd assume power over the world.

Rose Crowley subsequently fell into another trance and channeled *The Book of the Law*, said to confirm that Crowley was the new Lord of the New Aeon. The work was profoundly disrespectful to other spiritual leaders and religious orders. It includes lines such as "With my Hawk's head [i.e., Horus] I peck at the eyes of Jesus. . .I flap my wings in the face of Mohammed." Crowley was certain that he had received a major initiation and was ready to take over the world. Once Crowley became the Antichrist, humanity would begin the seven years of tribulation foretold in the Bible. It is of little surprise that this position was not accepted by the Christian church. However, this did not stop Crowley.

The self-appointed archenemy of Jesus Christ died in 1947,

never seeing the End he had envisioned. Addicted to drugs, in financial and physical ruin and without the groupies and apostles he had once attracted, Crowley passed away quietly, out of character for the man who had proclaimed himself the Antichrist and had planned to rule the world.

While the world didn't end, it seemed like it would at any time, since the planet was facing the worst turmoil ever experienced.

In the next chapter, we'll see how Doomsday prophecies burgeoned during the time that the world was at war.

Nation shall rise against nation,
and kingdom against kingdom.
—LUKE 21:10

5
THE WORLD AT WAR

$\mathcal{W}$ars, especially those that are billed as the "war that will end all wars," are looked upon with overwhelming fear. Wars bring about the deepest questioning of human existence.

Among the questions that arise are: What are we fighting for? Will this be the final war? Who is really right when so many innocents are killed? We wonder if any bloodshed can be worth it. And whether we might be witnessing the beginning of the Tribulation and of the biblical End.

In the upheaval of the Revolutionary War and its aftermath, scores of Doomsday prophets surfaced, gathering apostles and predicting the End. The War of 1812 was the catalyst for the movements of William Miller, Joseph Smith and other Doomsday religions.

Many people believed that the Civil War was the final act for humanity. What else could it mean when brother was killing brother? The war spawned many new religions, as well as searches for spiritual meanings in the paranormal.

Charles Taze Russell, founder of the Jehovah's Witnesses, announced that the End would come sometime between 1914 and 1918, the years that many countries were at war. Russell explained the basis for this belief in *Thy Kingdom Come*, the third volume of his *Studies in the Scriptures*. In the book, he told of the "harvest" time that would last 40 years, "until the overthrow of the professedly Christian Kingdoms, really kingdom of God in the earth. . ., the Terminus of the Times of the Gentiles." He foretold of the Jews returning to Palestine during this harvest period. The overthrow, he explained, could be clearly seen in the global troubles of the time, including the unrest in many European nations. He promised that, unlike his previous End Time prophecy, this one would result in an End seen by all of humanity.

The good news for the Witnesses was that, although the world's population would be purged, the faithful would survive (always a successful way to gather new followers). Russell supported the End Times prophecy based on measurements from the Great Pyramid at Giza, as discussed in chapter 1.

When the United States declared war, the Witnesses agreed that Russell's prophecies were correct: It was the beginning of the End, and Jehovah would be returning shortly. Russell announced that everything was on schedule, with a slight revision: The End would come in 1918, when a force unknown to humanity would produce the Battle of Armageddon, shortly followed by the Rapture of the entire church. (Russell never lived to see this final End Times prediction fail. He died on October 31, 1916.)

Scientist and seismographer Alberta Porta developed the first really big End Times scare of the twentieth century in the early 1920s. Porta correctly foretold the occurrence of massive storms and earthquakes around the earth—events she attributed to the forthcoming alignment of planets in our solar system. With the alignment, she believed, there would be such a gigantic gravitational pull that the entire planet would be thrown off kilter. This concept would later be known as the Jupiter effect.

During the years of World War I, many began to study the work of the prophet Nostradamus. He seemed to leave nothing to speculation regarding war and the end of the world. His magical writings seemed to foretell the American Revolution, the Civil War, World Wars I and II, the Yom Kippur War, and the ultimate of all conflicts, World War III. As evidence of the latter, disciples quote quatrain C9Q55:

C9Q55:
A horrible war which is being prepared in the West,
The following year the pestilence will come,
So very horrible that young nor old,
nor animal (may survive).

During World War II, both the Allied and the Axis forces used Nostradamus's prediction as propaganda to declare that each army would overthrow the other. Russell Chandler, author of a comprehensive history entitled *Doomsday*, writes that Adolf Hitler began stretching Nostradamus's obscure lines well beyond the intended deciphering, even though many believed that the stanzas actually foretold the downfall of the Third Reich.

Daniel Cohen, author of *Waiting for the Apocalypse*, explains that Hitler's minister of propaganda, Joseph Goebbels, went further. Goebbels is said to have composed fake verses and then instructed the Luftwaffe to drop thousands of the "Nostradamus leaflets" over Belgium and France throughout 1940. They indicated that Germany was foretold by the great prophet to be the supreme victor of the war. Therefore, the resistance forces should give up since it had been preordained that they would never win.

Cohen recounts how the British used some reverse propaganda of their own. They countered the psychological warfare by dropping Nostradamus's original (or slightly altered) predictions—with an Allied slant, of course—in the same area.

Could Nostradamus's predictions directly or indirectly have contributed to their fulfillment? Does predicting the future actually influence it? These are questions that Chandler, Cohen and other experts ponder. Chandler writes, "We must take seriously the idea that prophecies may be at least partially self-fulfilling because hearers take them seriously."

THE FATIMA AND OTHER MARIAN PROPHECIES

Many people believe that the Virgin Mary, mother of Jesus, is providing special notice that the End of the world is forthcoming. Called Marian prophecies, visions of the Virgin Mary, like UFO sightings, have been increasing since the early nineteenth century, especially in times of national strife. Many consider the signs to be warnings that the End is near. Christians relying on the Book of Revelation believe that there will be signs from God that the End is near although the majority do not tie the Marian visions directly to the Second Coming.

Psychologists point out that while UFO sighters are typically middle-aged couples living in rural areas of the country (we'll talk more about UFOs and the End in chapter 7), those who first see the Blessed Virgin Mary are usually young females from poor Catholic families.

On May 13, 1917, while Europe was at war, a beautiful lady from Heaven appeared to three girls between the ages of 10 and 13 who were out in a cornfield near the tiny town of Fatima in Portugal. The lady reappeared on five subsequent occasions over a period of six months. (There were other reports from the area, unbeknownst to the girls, that UFOs were sighted during the time.)

On the last appearance, the lady told the girls that she was to be called "Our Lady of the Rosary." She declared that a shrine should be built in her honor. She instructed them to recite the Rosary daily. She also shared a prophetic secret that is still being discussed and examined today.

During World War I, two of the children died having never divulged the secret. Lucia Santos, the third child to see the vision, was forever moved by it and became a Carmelite nun. Santos wrote two accounts of the visions in 1936-7 and 1941-2, and by permission of the Catholic church's authority, she was allowed to reveal a part of the secret the Lady of the Rosary gave her.

The prophecy of Our Lady of Fatima was produced in three parts and has been called the Threefold Message of Fatima. Its instructions included practicing Penance, reciting the Rosary and being devoted to the Immaculate Heart of Mary. But there was more. Some people believed that the information in the third portion could change the world, it was that significant. Yet, the Vatican has kept some of it under wraps because it believed that Catholics were not ready for it or possibly it was too earthshaking.

According to the girls who saw the visions, the first two prophecies, or parts, were of hell and the horrors of World War II (this was 1917). The third part was scheduled to be unveiled in 1960 or when the time was right. Yet 1960 came and went and the Vatican didn't let the news out of the bag. In 1963, however, the German newspaper *News Europe* published the alleged text that concerned the End. It contains many of the same alarming words as the Book of Revelation concerning doom and destruction, pestilence and plague. Some people contend that it foretells the date of World War III. The prophecy, as it related to the future, reads in part:

> A great war will break out in the second half of the twentieth century. Fire and smoke will fall from heaven, and waters of the oceans will become vapors. . .Millions and millions of men will perish. . .and those who survive will envy the dead. The unexpected will follow in every part of the world, anxiety, pain and misery in every country.

Other sources contradict the newspaper's account and say that the third part of the prophecy is still undisclosed. Some say it is trivial and that far too much has been made out of the revelation already. To this day, the Vatican has not officially released the third portion of what the Virgin Mary is said to have told the girls.

The visions of the Blessed Mother are not confined to illiterate children in cornfields and are becoming more regular. Generally, the Marian vision consists of the appearance of a luminous woman identified as the Virgin Mother. Sometimes she speaks; sometimes she doesn't. Typically, as with Fatima, she asks followers to pray for a more devout life. The Catholic church investigates most vision reports. Inquests often take years and can be compared to our government's bureaucratic investigations. So far, it has only decreed a few to be genuine; one of these is the Fatima vision.

The Church says these are not UFOs or ghosts but religious apparitions. They are a mystical phenomenon permitted by God. Those that the Church has authenticated have occurred in Guadalupe, Mexico (1531), Paris, France (1830), La Salette, France (between February 11 and July 16, 1858), Knock, Ireland (August 21, 1879), Fatima (1917); Beauraing, Belgium (November 29, 1932 to January 3, 1933) and Banneaux, Belgium (1933).

The sightings of Marian visions have increased in recent years, but they are not only the phantoms of New Age prophets or devoted Catholics. In 1970, more than three hundred apparitions appeared to Veronica Leucken, who lives on Long Island, New York. In 1988, parishioners of the St. John Neumann Roman Catholic Church, in Lubbock, Texas, encountered a Marian apparition. Depending on one's beliefs, these too may be signs of the End. According to some New Agers, the Marian visions are more than God's messenger. They are angels who want humans to know that we are not alone and will be safe in the disasters that lie ahead in the year 2000 and beyond.

Michael Grosso, an expert on supernatural visions and the author of *Frontiers of the Soul*, says that at the time of the Fatima prophecy, "crowds of witnesses were seeing globes of light in the sky, hearing rocketlike sounds, and so forth." The girls in the cornfield, however, swore that the vision was the Virgin Mary.

In 1968, there was a spectacular Marian apparition in Zeitoun, a suburb of Cairo, in the vicinity of St. Mary's Coptic Church. This time there were more than three uneducated children to testify to the appearance. The visions were seen over a 14-month period beginning April 2, 1968. On June 8, 1968, the vision lasted more than seven hours. Thousands witnessed the dazzling apparitions of a goddess figure; many captured the apparition on film. Miraculous cures were reported. This occurrence still remains to be explained.

Closer to home and more recently, hundreds of thousands of people have been flocking to a muddy farm field in Conyers, Georgia, to wait for, listen to and possibly see a vision of the Virgin Mary. It has been reported that she's visited the farm on the 13th of every month since 1990, according to farm owner Nancy Fowler.

Supposedly, the Blessed Mother, as explained by Fowler, who sees the visions, is disgusted with Catholics because they haven't been following her Fatima message of praying and believing in God and opposing abortion. During some of the events, visitors have claimed to see a cross in the sky; many have tried to photograph it, but to no avail. Some of the devout say that the sun begins to spin on its axis and beams of light shoot into the house at midday when the Virgin Mary is about to enter it. Fowler meets the Blessed Mother in a pine-paneled "apparition room." John Haber, a spokesperson for the farm corporation, called Our Loving Mother's Children Inc., says that it's no coincidence the number of visitors is increasing. "We are in the very last times" he told a newspaper reporter in 1994, "and Blessed Mary is appearing in order to try to bring her flock back to Jesus." Haber explains that he believes something special is definitely happening, since people are being transformed and purified.

Those who think of visions from a religious perspective believe that they are the goodness of Christ giving hope and a visible sign of his return. To those who verify the visions, Mary's authority as a messenger of Jesus cannot be denied; she brings about transformations for those who profess to see her. Psychologists, however, question the visions. Some suggest that they may be brought about by collective anxiety about the forthcoming millennium. Grosso says, "The destructive potential facing our planet, from nuclear war to AIDS, is inciting a global pattern of psychic phenomena."

Psychologists tell us not to be surprised if in these difficult times, there are more reports of this nature, including more visions of Mary. They speculate that the increase is connected to the destructive potential facing the planet and the poor condition of our economy. Similar visions were also reported near the end of the last millennium, and when crusaders reported seeing the New Jerusalem hovering in the sky as they returned to Europe.

Marian visitations have a unique function for Roman Catholics, religious experts point out. They represent the unfolding of biblical prophecies in a traditional, ritual way. Whether the visitation occurs on Long Island or in France, pilgrims flock for a view of the sight. For example, even dozens of years after the visitation at Lourdes in southwestern France, the grotto that was constructed there is still attended by believers. Each year, more than five million people visit the shrine, to pray, to seek guidance and to understand the messages of the End of time. They concur that the Virgin's appearances and messages have confirmed that the age of Mary has arrived. Because, you see, this is officially Doomsday, as outlined in the Bible, and the Virgin Mary is Jesus Christ's special emissary guiding us in the final days.

THE CARGO CULT LESSON

In preliterate or marginally literate societies during invasions or colonization or after wars, a unique phenomenon sometimes occurs whereby prophets of cargo cults predict the end of the world. The term "cargo cults" refers to the groups' belief that goods, or cargo, will be delivered to them from long-dead ancestors or spiritual beings, and thus they will be taken care of in a heaven on earth. According to a similar theory, the world will be delivered from Doomsday through the assistance of good-samaritan space aliens or even the hand of Jesus Christ. Sometimes, the groups are referred to by social scientists as "crisis" or "contact" cults. They follow a pattern similar to those of Christian-oriented sects as they wait for the end.

Because of World War II, more preliterate people were touched by industrialization than ever before. Cargo cults came to public notice in the late 1940s and 1950s, when news of "strange" tribal occurrences and rituals appeared in the tribes of the Melanesians, native inhabitants of South Pacific islands. The tabloids and magazines of the time may have considered them strange, but the cults' beliefs reflected the same pattern followed by Miller and others. The cargo cults just had a slightly different twist.

The tribes strongly believed that the cargo planes and ships that invaded their islands during World War II would return to bring Westernized goods and services. Some tribes built flimsy reed or palm temples in the shapes of airplanes, worshipped deities resembling Red Cross workers and soldiers and completed various rituals in order to provoke the spirits to bring deliverance. In some cases, the rituals were performed to chase away the foreigners remaining on tribal lands because it was believed that the gods or their honored ancestors would not return until the foreigners were gone.

Although the theories of cargo cults have been noted through history, especially during the years before 1000 A.D., cults were first documented in the South Pacific around 1880 in Fiji. They normally follow a particular pattern. Out of nowhere, a prophet appears and predicts that salvation from a terrible life is about to come (typically this is not someone who has been born into or has family within the tribe or group). This salvation may be envisioned as the return of the islanders' respected ancestors in boats, of gods coming from the skies in flying ships, or even of ships arriving by sea, loaded with consumer goods.

In one group after World War II, the desire for salvation and to return to a heaven was so strong that the self-appointed prophet ordered his apostles to perform specific rites to make those events happen. The prophet said it had been revealed to him that ships were coming, loaded with merchandise and goods unavailable on the island. The goods would include radios, clothing, furniture, canned foods, medical supplies and even jeeps. The prophet told his followers that these were gifts from their ancestors. There would be many more gifts as soon as the tribe was ready to receive them. Thus, they didn't need the things they already owned. The tribe was informed that in the prophet's vision, he had been told that their benefactors were great ancestors, not white-skinned Western soldiers or medical staff. The ancestors would also be returning to the island, although they had been dead since before anyone could remember. Because the goods would be coming in such abundance, the prophet directed that his followers build a warehouse in which to store the merchandise. They were also directed to construct a jetty so that the ship could arrive. They then were told to get themselves ready by dressing in their finest ceremonial attire—instructions reminiscent of William Miller's telling his disciples that it wouldn't be right not to wear white ascension robes when their powerful ancestors were about to take them to their final reward.

Although there are variations, the scenario above seems to be the foundation for most cargo cults. There is always at least one prophet, and sometimes several assistant prophets. Typically, the prophets are men, but women have on occasion filled the role. While the cargo normally is expected to be delivered by ship or through the air from the gods, one cult in the South Pacific built a primitive airstrip for the planes that would supposedly be piloted by their ancestors, so that the flying ships could land on the island. The runway was a crude, flat area outlined by sticks and covered by lava ash. Some cults have attempted to use their local currency to buy salvation in the form of a powerful, magical person. For instance, in the late 1960s, one group in Malaysia tried to buy President Lyndon Johnson. During World War II, another group wanted to buy FDR.

Cargo cult case studies often report the slaughtering of livestock and great ritual feasts. All supplies are used in preparation for the feasts, since once the ships and goods arrived, the community would not need to grow their own food. Additionally, other rituals were performed as shows of faith. They included abstinence from sex, separation of the sexes, rituals of sacrifice and taking money or valuable possessions into the sea or burning objects. Such actions are intended to show that the tribe is dedicated to the ancestors or gods who are expected to alleviate their poverty. This is a concept illustrated throughout history. The End Times agenda of the prophet Montanus included celibacy, living a poor but devoted life and awaiting the End.

Some social scientists theorize that the cults are a form of colonial rebellion in the disguise of a strange religion. During the McCarthy era, a Malaysian cargo cult called the Masigna Rule was accused of being involved in a Communist or Marxist plot. In all probability, the cults are a way of coping with bewildering changes and reflect a desire to return to fundamental morals.

Before World War II, the cargo cults lived simple lives with little pressure from outside sources. When colonization occurred, tribal members were used as laborers by the planters and traders and introduced to consumer goods.

In such cases, the lesson gleaned is that white people are extremely powerful, possibly even magical. Whites know how to organize police forces and church congregations and how to heal the sick and care for the dying. Whites claim there is a better world for those who are good in this lifetime, and in this other world, there will be peace, but only if their own rituals are followed.

Sociologists say that tribes may react as they do in part because they envy the power of Westerners. We are also told that these cults arise in times of extreme crisis, accompanied by widespread cultural and social disintegration. The end of a massive war is the perfect example. In the early 1950s, members of a cult on one Pacific island waited for weeks near signs painted with red crosses in the hopes that Red Cross planes would bring them food, medical supplies and basic necessities, as had happened during World War II.

What transpires when the long-awaited salvation doesn't come? When the group isn't saved or the god doesn't arrive with the cargo on the predicted day, the prophet sometimes stalls for time, stating that the previous date was intentionally false, a means of testing the group's faith. Or the prophet may claim that salvation had to be postponed because there was someone in the group who wasn't sufficiently devout. When the tribe assures the prophet that they do believe in the End, they are admonished to perform other rituals to summon the event. Then the group waits again.

Anthropologists explain cargo cults and other Doomsday sects as a way of coping with change. They help people come to terms with such stresses as the breakdown of the family unit, increased crime and loss of traditional values. Some groups, like the Fundamentalist Christians, seek to reinstitute a previous, more stringent, social and moral order.

JUST THE PLAIN TRUTH

World War I was over and the country was on a financial roll when Herbert W. Armstrong started the Worldwide Church of God (WCG). By 1930, with the country on the brink of the Depression, Armstrong was setting dates for the End.

He told his followers that they alone would be saved and raptured (an ancient word meaning transported) to the glorious walled city of Petra, south of Jordan. The rapture was to take place in 1936 (he later changed the date to 1943, then 1972 and finally 1975).

In 1934, Armstrong went on the air with the "Radio Church of God," transmitted directly from Eugene, Oregon. He began publishing *Plain Truth* magazine at that time too, and both the broadcast (now called "The World") and the magazine still have a global following.

When the date set for the End came and went, Armstrong didn't say "Sorry." Instead, he pointed a finger at the individual who supposedly had caused the cancellation of the rapture: Garner Ted Armstrong, Herbert W.'s son. It seems that Garner Ted, who was involved in a sex scandal, à la Jimmy Bakker and Jimmy Swaggart, had stopped the rapture from taking place with his immoral behavior. Garner Ted was "in bonds with Satan."

Garner Ted was shortly asked to leave the church, not for sexual indiscretions, but for committing the horrible crime of being liberal and too modern. He later opened his own church and collected many followers who were disappointed with the WCG.

Shortly thereafter, the Armstrong regime became riddled with swindles, financial indiscretions and other troubles similar to those experienced by other evangelical ministries in recent history. Nevertheless, the movement didn't die.

Armstrong's followers kept following, even through the last disconfirmation in 1975. It was at that time that Armstrong stopped predicting the End and argued that there were to be three resurrections of the dead instead. In the first, Jesus would return in the millennium as the leader of the worldwide true church. He would be the church's messiah. Then the "Resurrection of the Ignorant" was to take place, after the millennium, to enlighten the dense souls who were left. And third would be the resurrection of the sinners, after which time they would be "cast into a lake of fire." The WCG's game plan for getting to eternity is more explicit than many mainstream Christian theologies.

In the years since Armstrong's death in 1986, the church he founded has continued, although more slowly than before. It now has an estimated 87,000 members worldwide. There is new leadership, and the dogma has changed. Currently, Armstrong's statement that humans will someday become God has "officially been declared obsolete." The church is no longer, publicly at least, predicting when D day will happen.

In 1988, Martin C. Filipello, a former member of the WCG, began preaching Armstrong's version of the End when he began another sect, the Church of God Philadelphia Era. He accused the current leaders of the WCG of being corrupt and "laced with doctrinal error." Filipello, like his mentor, believed that he was a modern-day "Elijah sent to purify God's church." He believed that he and Armstrong were the "two witnesses" spoken of in Revelation 11 and Zechariah 4.

Filipello predicted that in January 1988, Armstrong would rise from the grave to lead believers through this time of Tribulation. So far Armstrong's bones remain at rest in his grave, but loyal supporters are still hopeful that Armstrong and Filipello will lead the way in the coming millennium.

THE END AND NUCLEAR WINTER

As the world moved from the monumental plunder and destruction of the first World War into that of the second, new

Doomsday scenarios were envisioned. With the world gone crazy, it was easy to believe that humankind was living in the final days, especially with the invention of the atomic bomb.

Even into the sixties, American children would practice "drop drills" in order to protect themselves in the event of a nuclear attack. Would the end be precipitated by someone's finger on a nuclear trigger? Though the fallout shelters are now part of the past and the cold war has defrosted, the threat of an end-all war is still present.

Only a few year ago, the fingers hovering above nuclear detonators were either Soviet or American. Even in the most frigid moments of the cold war, we felt somewhat safe since both sides attempted to judiciously consider the effects of nuclear war, even though the threats often didn't sound that way. Well, we're not any safer since the cold war ended. That false sense of security, too, is of the past.

Since the breakdown of the Soviet Union, the powers that could produce the ultimate bad day have proliferated. Shortly, government sources say, more than 25 nations will have nuclear weapons capabilities. In the forties, Sir Winston Churchill said, "The atomic bomb is the Second Coming in wrath."

Scientists, environmentalists and politicians (and scads of concerned citizens worldwide) worry about "loose nukes," a term coined by Dima Litvinov, the head of Greenpeace in Russia, to indicate that nuclear bomb potential is out of control. Litvinov worries about "loose nukes walking around Russia" and with good reason. The former Soviet Union has reported several disappearances of highly enriched uranium (a key component of bombs). Recently, Russia disclosed the theft of two fuel rods containing uranium from the site of the Chernobyl power plant (where a nuclear meltdown occurred in 1986). *Time* magazine correspondent Bruce W. Nelan has characterized such incidents as the first symptoms of a nuclear plague spreading throughout Europe. "After years of scares and false alarms" Nelan wrote in

August of 1994 ". . .German police have in the past four months uncovered four cases of smuggled nuclear materials that could actually be used to make an atom bomb." The materials, although intercepted, were destined for the black market, to be sold to the highest bidders.

Leonard Spector, a nuclear-proliferation expert with the Carnegie Endowment for International Peace, explains that in "the old days, it took 10 years from the time a country wanted a bomb to when they would actually get a bomb. Now countries may be able to suddenly jump ahead." Those countries that now hold bomb makings include such "rogue states" as North Korea, Algeria, Iraq and Iran.

Obviously, the threat of nuclear war didn't disappear when the Soviets went out of business. That's a big worry on the minds of many. The Central Intelligence Agency and the Pentagon are attempting to counter the risks of nuclear proliferation. The theft from Chernobyl, still one of the most dangerous spots on the face of the earth, typifies just how far people and governments will go to get bomb supplies. And even more than a half century after the holocaust of Hiroshima, we don't have to listen very carefully to hear the Doomsday clock going ticktock, ticktock.

With the threat of war looming over us, many men, women and children have found hope in God and Jesus Christ. It was during some of the darkest years of the cold war that religion enjoyed a renaissance that is still with us today.

IS THE EUROPEAN COMMUNITY AN END TIMES PROPHECY FULFILLED?

Many believe the common market of European nations, or the European Community (EC), was an economic lifesaver. Many believe it is a way to instill a resurgence of faith in democracy through world government. But wait! Once more, those who believe that we're at the Eve of Destruction see a world government, including the establishment of the EC, as yet another fulfillment of End Times prophecies. They believe that when the EC joined together, this was one more tick on the Doomsday clock as the hands moved closer to twelve.

The concept of one world government isn't new. Some world leaders, including former president George Bush, see it as the ultimate vision of peace. Some envision it as part of a utopian future that includes redistribution of wealth on a global scale. The idea is hotly opposed by many, including Christian leader Pat Robertson, founder of the Christian Broadcasting Network. In his book, *The New World Order*, he claims that turning over personal wealth to the distribution system would bankrupt the average American.

There are conservative Christians in the United States and Europe who see the European Community as the revival of the Roman Empire as outlined in the Scriptures (Dan. 7). Opponents of this concept point out that the Bible says that the new Roman Empire (in power at the End) will be made up of ten nations, while the current EC has twelve. Those Christians who label the EC as the fulfillment of the prophecy believe this will change, however, and that two of the members will drop out before the End.

John Paul II, the Roman Catholic Pope, is reportedly fearful of the ramifications of the EC, the power it could wield and of the End it could foretell. Christians explain that the Pope's concerns mirror the dire warning of evangelical Protestants. Malachi Martin, in his book *The Keys of This Blood*, says that John Paul II sees Russia as the prime catalyst of geopolitical change and expects to see more movement toward a one-world government. Martin says that John Paul II appreciates that we are living in the final stages of history before the return of Jesus Christ. Will the Pope, who has traveled more and brought more people of all faiths together than any other leader of the Roman Catholics, give religious assistance to the EC? Martin says no. He writes that John Paul II "has already put all nations on notice as to why their most elaborate plans for a 'greater European space,' for the 'common European house from the Atlantic to the Urals,' and for the totally 'new world order' will [not] and cannot succeed."

Martin explains that the papacy is "concerned with the material conditions of man's life and habitat, and with the 'human' values needed to ensure its pleasantness, exclusive of Christianity's moral law, deriving none of its motivations from Christian beliefs and incorporating none of the practices Christianity has always regarded as essential and obligatory for men and women." Martin says the Pope's objections to the EC are, "[b]riefly and graphically put, [that] nowhere in the intricate plans for the new or the renewed Europe is the God of Christians affirmed, adored and cultivated." Supposedly, the Pope believes that the Europe of the future is godless, just as large segments of Europe are already godless and without religion.

Apparently, the Pope also believes that a united EC of great power is in the future for the world, and insists that he will live to see the return of Jesus to save his church and redeem mankind. However, he contends that he will not help unite Europe with a "godless" government. His goal is to save the church, not extend the godlessness of Europe and the world.

Religious experts like Martin indicate that there are those forces within the Vatican ready to replace John Paul II, already in his seventies, who may not live to achieve his goal of saving the church. Christians wonder if his successor will or if, in fact, the Pope in power during the Tribulation will be the ruler of the new Roman Empire as foretold in the Book of Daniel.

Many people believe that with the increased economic power of the EC, America will lose its power and become a second-rate force in the world. This, too, would be a fulfillment of End Times prophecies. Former French president Giscard d'Estaing, in a conversation with Henry Kissinger quoted in *Forbes* magazine, said, "By the year 2010, the entity that is Europe will be number one in the world's economy. The U.S. will be second, China third and Japan fourth."

Why the hubbub over the growth of the EC? Those who predict Doomsday see it as the revival of the Roman Empire (perhaps headquartered at the Vatican), destined to be headed by a charismatic leader. They believe that this popular dictator will dazzle the world and bring great wealth and power to Europe. They believe that this leader will also be the Antichrist, the most feared man of all time.

According to Evangelicals, the Antichrist is waiting out there to assume his throne. In the Bible, this individual who will rule in the End Days before the great battle between good and evil is waged will be called the King of Babylon, Little Horn, Man of Sin, Son of Perdition, Beast and Antichrist. Best-selling author Hal Lindsey (*The Late Great Planet Earth* and *Planet Earth—2000 A.D.*) explains that the Antichrist will initially be considered a great humanitarian and perform many miracles and solve world problems. Once the world's population is hoodwinked, he will become ruthless and make the atrocities of Adolf Hitler and Josef Stalin seem like child's play. Lindsey explains that if we keep on the path now taken and continue to espouse New Age theories and the occult, the population of the world will not be fazed by the miracles performed by this diabolic dictator. The Antichrist, some Christians believe, is alive and well this very minute. They insist that he is about to ascend the throne of the one-world government and is perhaps getting ready to assume power over the EC while you're reading this.

In the next chapter we'll look at the growth of the Fundamentalists and the return to basic Bible religions.

And whosoever was not found written
in the book of life was cast to the lake of fire.
—REVELATION 20:15

6
BACK TO BIBLE BASICS
AND BEYOND

There's a quip circulating among Fundamentalist sects concerning how best to prepare for Doomsday. It seems that one day, word reached a flamboyant television ministry that Jesus Christ had indeed returned. The television crew, the office staff and everybody at the studio were dumbstruck. Finally, one member had the wherewithal to barge into the office of their charismatic preacher and ask, "What advice can you give us, Brother Jones? What should we do, Brother Jones?" Brother Jones straightened his tie, grabbed a Bible and headed toward the door. "I don't know 'bout you, but when I meet Jesus, I want Him to see I've been busy!"

History tells of other zealous groups who believed that the End was at hand. Some left jobs and gave away all of their possessions. Living off the charity of others, they stayed very busy teaching the gospel as they kept an eye out for the End.

Today, many Fundamentalist groups are beehives of activity, speaking to groups and telling about their faith in Christ and the Second Coming. The increase in Fundamentalist sects has been well publicized in the press, and whenever you click the TV remote control through the channels, at any hour of the day or night, you're likely to find a cable program celebrating Christianity and Christ's return. The growth of Fundamentalism will be the focus of this chapter. However, we'll also listen in on what an orthodox Jewish sect is saying. . .because many in the group already believe that the messiah is here, now.

A BIT OF HISTORY

In the beginning of the twentieth century, there was a division between the mainline liberalism and conservative orthodoxy of Christian religion. In 1909, *The Fundamentalist*, a republication of an 1895 Niagara Bible Conference proposal, listed the five basic points of doctrine that one had to believe in if one were to be a Christian. They included:

1] The absolute truth of the Bible
2] The virgin birth of Jesus
3] The substitutionary atonement
4] The physical resurrection of Jesus
5] Jesus's imminent return to earth

Fundamentalism, according to the Reverend George Mather and the Reverend Larry A. Nichols (*Dictionary of Cults, Sects, Religions and the Occult*), was originally embraced by Presbyterians and Baptists. The groups wished to raise their voices in protest against modernists who had adopted theories such as Darwinism and liberalism of the time. These attributes of Fundamentalism became popularized throughout the Christian world in 1925, when William Jennings Bryan (1860-1925) prosecuted John T. Scopes, a Dayton, Tennessee, schoolteacher, who taught evolution in the public school system.

The term *Fundamentalism* is now applied to various conservative Christian sects that continue to reject any liberalism. This is, of course, liberalism as they see it. Some groups believe that it is too permissive (and thus intolerable) for members to dance, go to parties and/or participate in celebrations, including the Christmas holidays and especially Halloween (a day supposedly dedicated to witchcraft and the occult).

Even within the Fundamentalist groups, there are divisions of convictions. Some groups are praised, honored or belittled by being known as hyper-Fundamentalists, and pseudo-Fundamentalists, new Evangelicals and establishment Evangelicals. Then there are the right-wing Evangelicals, the middle-ground Evangelicals and the left-wing groups.

The term *Fundamentalism* has, in some circles, changed from meaning a doctrine based on a literal interpretation of the New and Old Testaments into a somewhat derogatory term. In some circles, it injects an image of anti-intellectualism. Some conservative Christians have therefore elected to call themselves Evangelicals. For simplicity's sake, we'll use "Fundamentalist" as an umbrella term to include all conservative Christians.

The Fundamentalist folks don't go around wearing sandwich boards with "The End Is Near" scribbled in 10-inch letters. Generally, they don't go on hunger strikes. Typically, they don't stand on soapboxes (at least most don't) and scream out dire threats of forthcoming doom taken from the Scriptures.

Some Fundamentalists rarely talk about their religion. Others go out of their way to promote their path to God, quoting Bible passages and reinforcing their prophetic statements with

Scripture messages that seem beyond the pale, especially when
they're trying to convert disbelievers. But as we've already seen,
those who predict D day's coming in or around the year 2000 are
not necessarily radical misfits nor Hollywood-style wackos. Often
they are co-workers, college roommates or members of the family
next door or across the street.

We live in a tremendously perplexing time. Since 1945 and
the development of the atomic bomb, humanity has had the means
by which to obliterate itself. Nuclear winter and global warming are
two good bets on how we might do it, according to Doomsday do-
it-yourselfers. Many people feel that the world is so messed up,
gone so hopelessly awry, that there's no possibility we'll be around
to collect Social Security checks, to say nothing of the prospects
for our children.

HEAVEN HELP US NOW

One can almost feel the apocalyptic thinking in the air. This is
especially brought home when some cults fulfill their own prophecies
of the end, such as David Koresh's Branch Davidians and the Swiss
sect called the Order of the Solar Temple (or the Cross of the Rose).
Most experts on biblically-based survivalists groups say we'll see more
of them springing up as we approach the turn of the century.

As we approach that fateful 2000, psychologists explain
that images stored in the unconscious may begin to haunt us.
The religious Fundamentalists translate cryptic verses in the
Bible's apocalyptic texts and relate them to thermonuclear
Armageddon. Some even point fingers at their favorite candidate
for the Antichrist.

The Doubting Thomases and Tonyas say that the times have
always been perplexing. For instance, in the fourteenth century,
various European Doomsayers were certain that it couldn't get any

worse—the black plague was spreading and the winter was entirely too cold, resulting in famine and widespread death from overexposure. It had to be the End. Even Rudolph I, the German king and ruler of the Holy Roman Empire, is believed to have said that the order of the seasons and the laws of the elements had fallen again into eternal chaos, and the end of the human race was feared. However, once the plague subsided, the dead buried and new crops harvested, thus taking the populace's mood and the economy out of the dumps, the predictions faded.

Even so, it does seem that there are more cults, sects and religious radicals than ever before. This supposed proliferation is often cited by Fundamentalists as evidence that the Bible prophecies are coming true.

The more conservative Christians quote Jesus Christ when He warned, "Take care not to be misled. Many will come in my name saying, 'I am He' and 'The time is at hand.' Do not follow them." But how can one know if this is really the End? While most Fundamentalists and evangelical Christians believe we're living in the End Times, others point out that there's no real way to be sure. Therefore, even in Christian circles, these questions are tough nuts to crack.

HAVE THEY BEEN RAPTURED?

Christian Fundamentalists find hope in Isa. 58:11: "And the Lord shall guide these continually, and satisfy thy soul in drought." And in Luke 21:36, where the apostle says followers must pray and follow His words, "in order that you may have the strength to escape these things that are about to take place, and to stand before the Son of Man." Most Fundamentalists believe they will not have to suffer through the seven terrible years of the Tribulation when the really bad stuff starts to come down.

Some Fundamentalists do preach in general terms as to when the End will arrive, but most look to the Scriptures quoted above for guidance and relate the words of the prophets and Jesus to what's going on today. According to some, God doesn't want His children, those who really believe, to be scared or hurt in the crossfire. Therefore, Fundamentalists believe that they've got an escape clause in their "contracts." It is known as the Rapture, an ancient word meaning to be transported. It is from the following Scriptures that many Christians glean hope that they'll avoid the real mess, the seven years of Tribulation, which usher in the End.

In 1 Cor. 15:51, Paul writes:

Behold, I tell you a mystery. We shall not all sleep, but we shall all be changed, in a moment, in the twinkling of an eye, at the last trumpet; for the trumpet will sound, and the dead will be raised imperishable, and we shall be changed.

Another passage from the Bible that Fundamentalists believe promises that they will be transported is found in 1 Thess. 4:13-18. In this Scripture, Paul is telling the Thessalonians that when the Rapture happens, they will be reunited with their dead. Christ assures that the dead will precede us, the living who are left after the terrible years of the Tribulation.

But we do not want you to be uninformed, brethren, about those who are asleep, that you may not grieve, as do the rest who have no hope. For if we believe that Jesus died and rose again, even so God will bring him those who have fallen asleep in Jesus. For this we say to you by the word of the Lord, that we who are alive, and remain until the coming of the Lord, shall not precede those who have fallen asleep. For the Lord Himself will descend from heaven with a shout, with the voice of the archangel, and with the trumpet of God; and the dead in Christ shall rise first. Then we who are alive and remain shall be caught up together with them in the clouds to meet the Lord in the air, and thus we shall always be with the Lord. Therefore, comfort one another with these words.

To promise followers that there will be plenty of room when they are Raptured, John 14:1-4, is quoted:

Let not your heart be troubled: ye believe in God, believe also in me. In my Father's house are many mansions: if it were not so, I would have told you. I go to prepare a place for you. And if I go and prepare a place for you, I will come again, and receive you unto myself; that where I am, there ye may be also. And whither I go ye know, and the way ye know.

Imagine a newspaper headline reading "Millions of Christians Raptured by Jesus." According to the Fundamentalists, we could read such words at any time. Most believers and their ministers are not impetuous enough to offer a date; too many have been off-target before, and date-setting is potentially disappointing.

Some Fundamentalists do hedge their bets by quoting the parable found in Luke 21:29, where we read:

Behold the fig tree and all the trees; as soon as they put forth leaves, you see it and know for yourselves that summer is now near. Even so you, too, when you see these things happening, recognize that the kingdom of God is near. Truly I say to you, this generation will not pass away until all things take place. Heaven and earth will pass away, but My words will not pass away. Be on guard, that your hearts may not be weighted down with dissipation and drunkenness and the worries of life, and that day come on you suddenly like a trip; for it will come upon all those who dwell on the face of all the earth. But keep on the alert at all times, praying in order that you may have strength to escape all these things that are about to take place, and to stand before the Son of Man.

Many Fundamentalist Christians believe that we are the generation referred to in this Scripture. They say that this parable means the terrible events leading up to the Rapture are like the leaves produced by the fig tree. And when the tree is filled with leaves, the End will come. They point out that many of the tragedies of our times, from famine and earthquake to AIDS and increased crime, are the leaves spoken of in this verse. They believe that only a few leaves are missing, and the fulfillment of biblical prophecies is nearly complete.

The End Timers alert followers to be ready, and they quote the Scriptures, especially 1 Thess. 5:1-2, which says, "Now brothers, about times and dates we do not need to write you, for you know very well that the day of the Lord will come like a thief in the night."

ONE SAVIOR, VARIED OPINIONS

Christianity teaches that there is one Savior, Jesus Christ, who will protect, love and save us in the End as He has done in the past. To accept Jesus Christ is therefore to accept the inevitability of Doomsday.

Some Fundamentalist groups, however, announce theirs is the "true" faith of Jesus Christ, and they alone know what will happen and when. They are sometimes so hostile toward other sects that they seem more like rabid politicians nearing the November elections than religious advocates.

Liberal Christians generally believe that the Scriptures allow for a great diversity of views. "Each individual Christian is a believer-priest, and he is related to God as a person," says Dave Breese, an evangelical crusader, board member of the National Association of Evangelicals and author of *Know the Marks of Cults*. Thus, while we wouldn't throw mud at our brothers or sisters, some Fundamentalists do exactly that even as they preach the dogma of the Second Coming.

Herbert Armstrong, the founder of the Worldwide Church of God and possibly the most widely known Fundamentalist of his time, expressed his theological opinions in a straight-line approach. "There is only one work that preaches the true gospel of the kingdom of God—the rule and the reign of God—to the nations," he wrote. "This is that work. Then those who have their part in this work and are converted must constitute the Church of God!

"Every other work rejects the message of Jesus Christ or else rejects His rule through His laws. There is no exception.

"Yes, this work is the work of the true church of God. All others are satanic counterfeits! It is time we come out from among them and become separate."

Herbert Armstrong believed that he alone was God's prophet, so we could forget about waiting for Christ's return, since He was here among us. Thus, he alone could predict the true date for the End. And in order to be in good standing with God, one must be a member of the true church, which of course was the WCG.

Sometimes Fundamentalists strike out on their own, insisting that they themselves are the Christ figure in the flesh and the longed-for Messiah whom the world must follow in these End Times. Joseph Newman is an example of a prophet of doom. He's been supporting the idea of the End for some time. In the early 1990s he appeared on a Mississippi television show (apparently buying a half hour's time) to tell the world: As all of the world's major religions, plus the psychics Edgar Cayce and Nostradamus and several other prophets, had foreseen, a messiah could come just before the End of the World, before the year 2000. He, Joseph Newman, was that messiah, or so his audience heard. Newman claimed that he was born of a virgin (yet two minutes later he began talking about his brother). As with other prophecy shows, Newman's announcement ended with a plea to send money.

When Fundamentalists become critical of other groups, self-proclaimed messiahs and even offshoots of their own sects appear. The groups are castigated by established faiths for being plagiaristic.

They are accused of adopting whatever religious doctrine is popular and will pull in members. They are accused of marketing religion and producing dogma to sway members from other sects.

This concept of taking the best from all religions and packaging it into one bundle of new-and-improved faith is what Dave Breese calls syncretism: "an attempt to gather together what some would call the best qualities of various religious points of view into a new and acceptable faith."

Some Fundamentalists become indignant on this topic, saying that syncretism is a favorite cult device and a creeping heresy, moving into many unexpected places. Almost invariably, the founders of fervent groups, we are told, rehash the existing concepts of orthodox faiths, saying they are the Messiah and theirs is the true church, and that only they can tell when the End will come and who will be saved. They clamor about the warmed-over doctrines found in Protestantism and Catholicism.

According to Breese, "Syncretism, the attempt to synchronize the Gospel of Christ with a godless world, is a deadly virus from which almost no institution recovers. This virus can infect us all and, becoming a plague, can carry us all away." Because of the spread of this disease, Breese asks, "When the Son of Man is come, will He find the faith on the earth?" Will he find any people?

It is predicted that because of the work of the false prophets, we're bound to witness more religious rip-offs and spin-offs in the Last Days. At the top of many Fundamentalists' list of religious copycats (and false prophets, preordained to come near the End) are the Christian Scientists.

They contended that founder Mary Baker Eddy snatched her philosophy from Phineas Parkhurst Quimby (1802-1866), a spiritualist and faith healer known as the guru of mind sciences and founder of New Thought. His ideas of mesmerism and spiritualism, we are told, were incorporated into her interpretation of the Bible. The Worldwide Church of God, Fundamentalists insist, yanked ideas from the Seventh-Day Adventists and stirred them with Judaism, adding extra thoughts on health and messianic theories.

The Jehovah's Witnesses have distributed billions of pamphlets announcing "God will destroy all false religion soon. . . God has given the world's religions a long time to prove what they are. Today we see their rotten fruitage all over the earth." And "the Bible shows that God's day for accounting is now at hand. For the honor of His own name, which has long been slandered, and for the eternal good of all persons who love righteousness, God must and will act." What will He do?

From "Has Religion Betrayed God and Man?" we read: "His inspired Word compares the world empire of false religion to a grossly immoral woman named 'Babylon the Great.' She is 'richly adorned,' living in 'shameless luxury.' In her is found the 'blood of all earth's slaughtered.' God sentences her to be 'burned with fire,' completely destroyed (see Revelation 17-18). This destruction will come from the very political powers that she has dominated for so long. What does this mean to you?"

TELLING THE TRUTH

How are we to tell if one is aligned with a cultic group, a false prophet or the "true" Christian church? According to Fundamentalists, this can be achieved by reviewing their belief in Jesus Christ and Salvation. If a group believes in Jesus Christ in the "right" way—that is, that He is the Savior—then they also believe in the Second Coming.

The Christian Science view of Jesus is:

* Jesus is the human who demonstrated Christ.

* Christ is the idea Truth, divine idea, the spiritual or true idea of God.

* Mary's conception of him was spiritual.

* Jesus was the offspring of Mary's self-consciousness communion with God.

* At the ascension of the human, material concept, or Jesus, disappeared, while the spiritual self, or Christ, continues to exist in the ethereal order of divine Science, taking away the sins of the world as the Christ has always done, even before the human Jesus was incarnate to mortal eyes.

* His resurrection was not bodily. He reappeared to his students, that is to their apprehension he rose from the grave—on the third day of his ascending thought! (From *Science and Health*, Mary Baker Eddy.)

The Mormons say:

* Jesus Christ is Jehovah, the first-born among the spirit children of Elohim to whom all others are juniors.

* He is unique in that he is the offspring of a mortal and of an immortal or resurrected and glorified, Father.

* He was the executive of the Father, Elohim, in the work of creation.

* He is greater than the Holy Spirit, which is subject onto him, but His Father is greater than He. (From *The Articles of Faith*, James E. Talmage; *Doctrine and Covenants* and *Doctrines of Salvation*, Joseph Smith.)

The New Age is definitely under suspicion by the Fundamentalists. Here's the philosophy of Jesus from the Theosophy point of view (a religious-based metaphysical movement started by Madame Helena Blavatsky, and Henry Steel Olcott):

* Jesus gave to the world fragments of teaching of value as basis for world religion, as did men like Buddha, Confucius, Pythagoras, etc.

* . . .at a certain stage in the career of Jesus, the latter was taken possession of by the great Teacher, the Bodhisattva of eastern tradition." (From *Modern Theosophy*, Hugh Shearman, 1952.)

* All men become Christs." (From *Is Theosophy Anti-Christian?*, Anne Besont)

The Church of Bible Understanding, also known as the Forever Family and headed by Art Traill, at one time had four thousand members; now it will no longer discuss the size of its membership. Members believe that the organization will play a key role in the End Times, although they will not say exactly what they are doing. Traill has hinted that he knows the exact date Christ will return. Unlike other Fundamentalist groups, however, the Church of Bible Understanding rejects the Trinity (Father, Son and Holy Ghost) and the deity of Christ. They believe that Jesus is a Savior, but he is not God, the Savior. Additionally, human beings are lost sinners and need salvation—according to the church's doctrine only.

As we've seen, Fundamentalists, while agreeing on principle that the End is about to finally happen, disagree on the cornerstones of dogma. Therefore, in their differing views of Jesus Christ, salvation and the ultimate judgment, they take various routes to the End. Let's look at salvation. In theological terms, salvation is the deliverance of a human being or human soul from the power or penalty of sin, of redemption.

* Those who practice the faith of Christian Science believe that salvation is the realization and demonstration of Life, Truth and Love as supreme over all, carrying with it the destruction of the illusions and delusion of mortal senses of sin, sickness and death.

* The Jehovah's Witnesses are told that the basis of judgment at the End of the 1,000 years before Christ returns is solely on the good works they perform during the millennium.

* The Unitarians believe salvation is based on character and developing moral values and spiritual insights.

* The Scientologists (founded by L. Ron Hubbard, 1911-1986) believe that salvation is the freedom from rebirth and karma and that all faiths are paths that lead to salvation.

* The United Church of Religious Science (also known as Religious Science and founded by Ernest Holmes, 1887-1960) is a mind/science religious group. They believe that there is no separation from God, ever. Therefore, the souls of believers never need to be saved. The only violation between God and human beings can happen when humanity stops believing in the oneness of God. They believe that Jesus understood the oneness and the laws of the universe. These laws are available to all followers, thus all can become like Christ.

The Fundamentalist group, Dawn Bible Students Associations, headquartered in New Jersey, believes we must work through these terrible times before the Second Coming will occur. The Day of the Lord will not come in a flash; rather "the trend of events of this Day of the Lord will be very deceptive to those not spiritually informed. . ." It will come sudden, as fire consuming chaff, "in comparison to the long ages past and their slow operation; but not suddenly as a flash of lightning from a clear sky, as some erroneously expect to anticipate that all things written concerning the Day of the Lord will be fulfilled in a twenty-four hour day." (Zeph. 2:2) They believe that the "Day" will come in spasms of pain, as in a series of convulsions more frequent and severe as the day draws on, until the final one.

Most Christian ministers, including Fundamentalists, point out that Christians are counseled not to judge one another. The Bible says, "Let us not therefore judge one another any more: but. . .rather, that no man put a stumbling block or an occasion to fall in his brother's way" (Rom. 14:13). We are given the choice to allow others to speak in their own minds and live in their own way. "Let every man be fully persuaded in his own mind" (Rom. 14:5). If it needs to be any clearer, 1 Corinthians 4:5 says, ". . .judge nothing before the time, until the Lord come, who both will bring to light the hidden things of darkness, and will make manifest the counsels of the hearts: and then shall every man have praise of God."

Ed Dobson and Ed Hindson, professors and the co-authors of *The Fundamentalist Phenomenon*, claim that Fundamentalists must join together in order to be a strong force in these most apocalyptic times. They write, "As Christians, we should remember that we are to be not only the Light of the world but also the Salt of the earth. Christian influence in society has always been the moral stability that has held this nation together."

Those who believe that they are being persecuted for their Fundamentalist or other Christian beliefs often go directly back to the source, the Bible, for hope, comfort and consolation. They also insist such persecution is in accordance with End Times prophecies. They quote Luke 21:12, 16: "But before all these [famine, earthquake and pestilence], they shall lay their hands on you, and persecute you, delivering you up to the synagogues, and into prisons, being brought before kings and rulers for my name's sake. . .And ye shall be betrayed both by parents, and brethren, and kinfolks, and friends; and some of you shall they cause to be put to death."

NO LONGER NECESSARY TO STAND IN LINE

"And the beast was taken, and with him the false prophet that wrought miracles before him, with which he deceived them that had received the mark of the beast, and them that worshipped his image. These both were cast alive into a lake of fire burning with brimstone" (Rev. 20).

According to religion's scorecard, the End will be a shut out for God, with the beast and false prophet ending up in the burning lake. When the dust of the Battle of Armageddon finally settles, according to the general consensus, we'll be living in a heaven on earth. Depending on which Scripture is quoted, here's what we're told it will be like:

* Christ will inherit the earth, the world's throne (Luke 1:32-3), which God promised to David would never cease on this earth (Sam. 7:13).

* During His physical time on earth, Jesus believed He was like a young nobleman going away (to Heaven) to be crowned and to return to earth after he became king (Luke 19:12-27).

* Throughout the New Testament, Jesus repeatedly said He would return (Matt. 24:27, 30-31, 42, 25:13; Mark 13:26; Luke 12:42-43, 17:24, 18:8, 19:12, 21:27; John 14:3, and others). Specifically in John

14:3, He said, "If I go and prepare a place for you, I will come again, and receive you unto myself, that where I am, there ye may be also." According to Zech. 14:3-4 and 1 Thess. 4:16, He will then be back on earth.

* The living Christ, with His Second Coming, will return with all the power and glory of Almighty God, as "King of Kings and Lord of Lords" (Rev. 19:11-21) to put down the rebellion of warring nations (Rev. 17:14) and establish God's world government for all nations (Dan. 2:44, 7:9, 13-14, 18, 22, 27; Isa. 9:7).

* The Second Coming, it will be a time to rejoice. Jesus Christ will be the reigning monarch on the planet for a thousand years. Jesus said, "And he that overcometh and keepeth my words unto the end, to him will I give power over the nations: and he shall rule them with a rod of iron. . ." (Rev. 2:26-27). And in Rev. 3:21, ". . .to him that overcometh will I grant to sit with me in my throne," and "we shall reign on the earth" (Rev. 5:10).

* The apostle John gives a preview of the joyous rule of a government headed by Jesus Christ. "And I saw thrones, and they sat up then, and judgment was given unto them. . .and they lived and reigned with Christ a thousand years."

* Christ is believed to be the King of Kings, all perfect in character, absolute in honesty, integrity and faithfulness. He is loyal and trustworthy and filled with concern for humanity. Yet when He reigns on Earth and possesses total power, He would never compromise His perfect law—the way of love for others.

Sketching a bright picture, Christians awaiting the Return believe that crime, sickness, disease, pain and hopelessness will be gone when that time comes. Poverty, abuse, persecution, hate and ignorance will be ousted.

What of the world in which we'll live like nobility? It will be filled with happy, healthy smiles. The wild animals will be tame and co-exist in harmony. Air will be crystal clean and the water from streams and rivers sweet and pure. The soil on the planet will be rich, black and fertile and, with the various earth changes to happen during the Tribulation, some Christians believe there will be more earth mass. The areas formerly uninhabitable or untillable will be fertile and hospitable. Flowers, gardens, crops and trees will grow in profusion. Humanity will no longer be at odds with each other.

In *The Wonderful World of Tomorrow—What It Will Be Like*, Herbert W. Armstrong, founder of the Worldwide Church of God wrote, there will be a "world filled with happy radiating humans, guided, helped, protected, and ruled by former mortals made immortal—and all the humans realizing that they, too, may inherit everlasting life in supreme happiness and thrilling joy. What a fabulous picture!"

For many faiths, that fabulous picture will only be peopled with those who foster similar beliefs. Therefore, in the Fundamentalists' millennium, there will only be those who have personally accepted Jesus into their lives. In the Mormon peace period of the millennium, only good Mormons will have a place of honor.

The Jehovah's Witnesses will only share their world with others who believe exactly as they do—that is, other Jehovah's Witnesses. These are the holy people, according to their conviction.

Must one be Mormon, Fundamentalist or a Witness in order to embrace the concept of world peace and freedom from want? Is there only one pathway to everlasting salvation? Denise L. Carmody, Ph.D., and John T. Carmody, Ph.D., professors of religion and authors of *Ways to the Center* explain, "There is a dictum in religious studies that he or she who knows just one religion knows no religion." Many still wonder at the narrow intellect of some sects.

A THOUGHTFUL FUTURE?

In all the Christian talk of prophecies, the Antichrist and the End, many voices describe a thoughtful future, including Jesus's. In 2 Peter 3:9, we learn that He does not want anyone to perish, and He is long-suffering. And in Matt. 24:42, Christ said "Watch therefore: for ye know not what hour your Lord doth come." Many mainstream Christians believe that as long as soothsayers predict dates and hours for His return, He will not return. If the enthusiasm for predicting the future continues and this statement is true, it may be a very long time before Christ returns.

The Scriptures say that Jesus Christ will not allow the word of soothsayers to fulfill his plans:

. . .I am the Lord who has made all things, who alone stretched out the heavens, who spread out the earth by myself, who foils the signs of false prophets and makes fools of divers, who overthrows the learning of the wise and turns it into nonsense, who carries out the words of his servants and fulfills the predictions of his messengers, who says of Jerusalem, 'It shall be inhabited,' of the towns of Judah, 'They shall be built,' and of their ruins, 'I will restore them' (Isa. 44:24-26).

In Jeremiah 18:7-10, we learn:

If at any time I announce that a nation or kingdom is to be uprooted, torn down and destroyed, and if that nation I warned repents of its evil, then I will relent and not inflict on it the disaster I had planned. And if at another time I announce that a nation or kingdom is to be built up and planted, and if it does evil in my sight and does not obey me, then I will reconsider the good I had intended to do for it.

Those Christians who relish End Times revelations often cite Amos 3:7 to justify the practice of date-setting: "Surely the Sovereign Lord does nothing without revealing his plan to his servants the prophets." However, they ignore the warning of the angel who brought the visions of the Last Day to the Apostle John in Rev. 22:18-19:

> For I testify unto every man that heareth the words of the prophecy of this book, If any man shall add unto these things, God shall add unto him the plagues that are written in this book.
> And if any man shall take away from the words of the book of this prophecy, God shall take away his part out of the book of life and out of the holy city, and from the things which are written in this book.

William M. Alnor, journalist, theologian and author of *Soothsayers of the Second Coming*, believes that such a formidable warning, shouldn't go unheeded. Alnor says, "There would not be soothsayers and unbiblical sensationalists today if a ready audience did not demand their teachings. Those who seek after unbiblical revelations and are not satisfied with studying God's Word are just as responsible for the Bible being discredited."

Alnor believes this behavior is anticipated in 2 Timothy 4:3, 4, where we read:

> For the time will come when men will not put up with sound doctrine. Instead, to suit their own desires, they will gather around them a great number of teachers to say what their itching ears want to hear. They will turn their ears away from the truth and turn aside to myths.

So when will He return? When is the Second Coming? In 1 Thess. 5:1-2, we read, "Now brothers, about times and dates we do not need to write you, for you know very well that the day of the Lord will come like a thief in the night." Matt. 26:64 says that at the end of the age, "you will see the Son of Man sitting on the right hand of the Mighty One and coming on the clouds of heaven."

In the caring voice of religious reason, the Drs. Carmody explain, "In a dark and troubled time (that is, in any historical time), saints and enlightened people save our beleaguered hope. Just one of them is stronger than all the rubbish, all the valid ground for cynicism. For a single really holy, really religious, really human person says that what we want and need is possible. We want and need light and love. Light and love are possible. By definition, light and love are buddha-nature and God. By saintly testimony, they are our center."

Religion, according to James Davidson, professor at Purdue University and co-author of *American Catholic Laity in a Changing Church*, will remain a vital dimension of American life through the 1990s and well into the next century. We need not fear. He says that our society will become no more secular than it is now and forecasts a strengthening of mainstream Protestant and Catholic groups. He also predicts that as we move toward the turn of the century, the religious right will lose favor with the masses, and its influence will be greatly diminished. We actually may tire of all the pessimistic End Times chatter—if the End does not come.

Isaac Bashevis Singer, the Polish-American Yiddish author, wrote, "Doubt is part of all religion. All the religious thinkers were doubters." There are many among the mainstream religious who doubt that the End is near or coming near to an earth you love. Many have doubts about the current thrust of Fundamentalist revivalists and their focus on an apocalyptic future. Yet the Fundamentalists who are preaching that old-time religion of fire, brimstone and a terrible End continue to draw great numbers of converts as they plan for a rapturous return.

Looking for the True Prophet

Christian leaders ask, How can Jews be so sure that the descendant of David is the true Messiah and not a false pretender, as foretold in the Bible? Clearly, there is no answer but that which is determined by personal and religious convictions.

In the search for the true Messiah, the Jews and Christians are in good company. The Mahdi, Arab for "he who is divinely guided" and who, in the Sunni Islam sect, is the restorer of faith, is joyfully awaited. It is believed that Mahdi will appear at the end of time to restore justice on earth and establish universal Islam. Among the Shiites, the concept of the Mahdi centers on the Imam. The Imam may be a human teacher of Shiite Islam, or he may be a mystical teacher ruling over various ages of time. The last of the mystical Imams will rule in secret but announce the end of time. When the Imam comes, as in other theories of messiahs, the Shiites will be recompensed for their sufferings.

Throughout Islamic history, many reformers have claimed to be the Mahdi, and at times rumors circulated that the Imam had begun the mysterious secret teachings. One was Muhammad Ahmad (1844-85), a Muslim religious leader in the Anglo-Egyptian Sudan. In 1881, Muhammad Ahmad declared that he alone was the Mahdi. All others were imposters. However, Muhammad Ahmad, the Messiah who held the power of God on his side, died a mortal death shortly after the fall of Khartoum. The British field marshal Lord Horatio Herbert Kitchener defeated Muhammad Ahmad's followers at Omdurman in 1898, and the end didn't come.

The Christian Scientists do not believe it will be Jesus Christ who'll reign in the Last Days. They believe that Jesus was a man, and men are mere matter. Matter (along with evil, sin and pain) does not exist. They believe that Jesus's mission on earth was to teach humanity that any and all sickness is an illusion. The Christian Scientist makes a sharp distinction between Jesus the man, teacher and missionary and Jesus Christ, who envelops a divine idea.

Mary Baker Eddy wrote in *Science and Health with Key to the Scriptures*, "Christ is the ideal Truth, that comes to heal sickness and sin through Christian Science, and attributes all power to God. Jesus is the name of the man who, more than all other men, has presented Christ, the true idea of God. . .Jesus is the human man and Christ is the divine idea; hence the duality of Jesus the Christ."

Christian Scientists believe that because the universe is God or the Spirit, and matter is a mere illusion, there is no specific direction to human history. There is no need for a transformation to occur in the future. We live in an illusion, and any trauma we might feel (or incur during the horror of the End) will of course be an illusion, too.

The End Times view of the Roman Catholic Church, found in *Catechism of the Catholic Church*, published by numerous agencies of the Vatican, provides a full account of Catholic beliefs relevant to the approach of the year 2000. This includes a strong message regarding the return of Jesus Christ.

Roman Catholics believe that before Christ's Second Coming, the church must pass through a final trial that will shake the faith of many. The persecution that accompanies a pilgrimage on earth will unveil the "mystery of iniquity" in the form of a religious deception. Catholics are told it will offer an apparent solution to their problems, but at the price of apostasy. The doctrine tells that this supreme religious deception will be the work of the Antichrist, a pseudo-messianism by which man glorifies himself in the place of God and of the Messiah.

According to the Catholic catechism, followers are taught: "The Antichrist's deception already begins to take shape in the world every time the claim is made to realize within history that messianic hope which can only be realized beyond history through the eschatological judgment. The Church has rejected even modified forms of this falsification of the kingdom to come under the name of millenarianism, especially the intrinsically perverse political form of a secular messianism."

At the End, the Catholic church will enter the glory of the kingdom of God through the final passover, when believers follow Jesus Christ in his death and Resurrection. They believe that the kingdom will be fulfilled, then, not by a historic triumph of the church through a progressive ascendancy but only by God's victory over the final unleashing of evil, which will cause his bride to come to heaven. (The church is the "Bride" of Christ: "He loved her and handed Himself over for her. He has purified her by his blood and made her the fruitful mother of all God's children.") It is God's triumph over evil that will be seen in the Last Judgment, after the final cosmic upheaval of this passing world.

In summary, regarding the End, the Catholic church believes:

* Christ the Lord already reigns through the church, but all the things of this world are not yet subjected to Him. It will take one last assault for the millennium to arrive.

* On Judgment Day, at the End, Christ will come in glory to achieve the definitive triumph of good over evil which, like the wheat and the tares, have grown together in the course of history.

* When He comes at the End of time to judge the living and the dead, the glorious Christ will reveal the secret disposition of hearts and will render to each man according to his works and according to his acceptance or refusal of grace.

Generally, mainstream religious beliefs regarding the Second Coming of Jesus Christ and the End can be summarized by the *Oxford Dictionary of the Christian Church*. It says:

Primitive Christianity believed the event (the End and return
of Christ) to be imminent and this belief has been revived
from time to time in the history of the Church. The
prevailing Christian tradition, while maintaining that our
Lord's word attests the certainty of a final General Judgment
which will mark the end of the present order and the entry
of redeemed humanity into the resurrection-life of heaven,
has been opposed to speculation as to the exact time and
manner of the coming.

It is believed that in the Judgment, humanity will be
confronted by the risen and glorified Christ. The supposition
that Christ, when He returned, would first reign for a long
period on earth (the Millennium) was held in some early
Christian circles, but it has not been generally followed.

However, as we move closer to the year 2000, more and more
traditional Christians are waiting for the End.

FUNDAMENTALISTS AND VISIONARIES

Fundamentalists are visionaries. They earnestly await the
return of Jesus Christ, salvation and the End. One must honor their
dedication and strength of belief, regardless of one's personal views.

Among those Fundamentalists who vocally support the
Doomsday concept is Jack Van Impe, affectionately known as the
"Walking Bible," whose church is headquartered in Troy, Michigan.
Van Impe believes the End will come in September 1999. "Signs
are happening with great rapidity before our very eyes. I believe the
president of the U.S.A. during the next eight years may face
horrendous decisions concerning World War III and even
Armageddon," he has said.

Charles Taylor's "Today in Bible Prophecy," a radio show
based in Huntington Beach, California, is transmitted globally via
communications satellites so that people around the world may

receive the message that we're in the tribulation years now. David Webber's Southwest Radio Church has predicted the End at various times within the past few years, broadcasting its message on over one hundred radio channels in the United States. Pat Robertson's Christian Broadcasting Network and the Trinity Broadcasting Network preach their Doomsday message through the use of cable TV, and in Houston, Hilton Sutton and his prophecy group keep a 24-hour D day hotline open.

Almost all Christian churches, from mainstream sects to Fundamentalists, agree that eventually Jesus Christ will return. The ones that have the strongest and most convincing beliefs in the End are those showing the most growth. The Assemblies of God church grew by nearly 120 percent from 1965 to 1989, and now has over 2.2 million members. The Seventh-Day Adventists have grown by over 90 percent in that same period. The Jehovah's Witnesses currently have more than 860,000 members. Many smaller Fundamentalist sects are finding that it is nearly impossible to fit all the believers into the church on Sunday .

Most fundamentalists preach the Gospel—the pure-and-simple, back-to-the-Bible basics. As one televangelist recently said, "You don't have to be a great theologian to figure it out. The End is nearing, and people know it. All any of us has to do is read the Scriptures and accept them for what they are."

The End of the world concerns more than the Fundamentalists. Some Hebrew sects, believing that they are the chosen people, insist that they have the answer to the End because the future includes their Messiah.

The Lubavitcher followers are currently experiencing Messiah fever. Some supporters even chose their Messiah, the 90-year-old Menachem Schneerson of Brooklyn, New York. However, since the Rabbi's stroke and subsequent death in 1994, there has been less faith that the Rabbi is the "Main Man." Yet more than ever, in Jerusalem and in enclaves throughout the world, there are those who scribble signs and wear buttons announcing "Welcome to the King." And they aren't talking about Elvis.

Believing that the End is here, they quote the liberation of Jerusalem, the gathering of the Jewish exiles from all over the world and the fall of the Soviet Union as verification of their prophecy. Rabbi Shlomo Riskin, dean of the Ohr Tora Institutions and chief rabbi of Efrat explains that "the dream of ultimate Redemption must be understood as the cornerstone of our faith." Quoted in the *Jerusalem Post*, Rabbi Riskin said, "In the Amida prayer, which we recite thrice daily, we speak of Jerusalem and the Ingathering as preceding the rebuilding of the Temple and the Messiah's rule. When we read the prophetic visions and see the renaissance and development of a lush and inviting Jewish homeland, we cannot but be inspired by the signs."

Like many Christians, the world's Jewish population is waiting for the Messiah. However, rather than coming from the Heavens, Jews believe that the Messiah will be a human descendant of David, "the Mighty God, the Father of Eternity and the Prince of Peace" (Isaiah 9:6,7). Rabbi Riskin explains, "Ultimately, the job of the Messiah is to gather the nations under the blanket of the One God, and to bring the world peace. If a gathering of the nations for the sake of peace is an explicit description of the messianic period, it clearly suggests something natural, human and recognizable." It may also be a clear indication that we have moved into an age where there will be many who insist that they are the Chosen Ones.

In the next chapter, we'll move from the age-old text of the Bible to the New Age prophets and find out what they have to say about the end . . . and any possibility of a future.

It's all in the mind, and we're it.

—MOIRA TIMMS, *BEYOND PROPHECIES AND PREDICTIONS*

7

IT'S IN THE STARS

What have the gurus of metaphysical thought said about the End? What are New Age teachers telling their followers? In this chapter, we'll hear opinions from the New Age prophets of the past and those of our time, including UFO-ers, astrologers, numerologers and other cult figures.

A GIANT LEAP FORWARD

Humanity is about to face a quantum leap forward. We are in the final generation of an ancient civilization. We are headed for the first generation of a new one. Whether we're ready or not, the future is waiting on the threshold of the millennium. These are the opinions shared by many New Age believers, who are anxiously awaiting what they expect will be the best times yet.

"Talk these days of a threshold, a watershed, a decisive epoch, a hinge of history, a countdown stage, a critical transition, an evolutionary leap, a crossroads—of humankind at a cusp—is of course the old coin of apocalypse burnished for millennium's end," writes Hillel Schwartz in *Century's End*. Like Schwartz, many believe that the breakdown of everything we hold near and dear on this planet will prove to be a breakthrough to the creation of a better world.

Theories from New Age camps regarding the End of the World do not originate only in places as hip as Malibu, California, or Sedona, Arizona. They have actually been with us since people began discussing ideas. One must remember that religion was once considered "new thought" and Christian teachings were heresy in ancient Roman times.

New Age thoughts are technically grouped in a school of philosophy called metaphysics. This branch of philosophy is concerned with the ultimate nature of existence and is often attributed to Aristotle. While Aristotle might have shivered at some New Age practices, from healing with crystals to reading auras, he may have approved of some of the more rational thoughts regarding Doomsday.

SCALLION'S SUPER-MEGA

Gordon Michael Scallion, called a New Age prophet by his followers, shares many of Edgar Cayce's theories regarding the finality of humankind. Like Cayce, Scallion also psychically predicted massive geological changes in the next few years.

Scallion doesn't just say there will be a big earthquake; he calls it the "super-mega quake." It will be so huge that our Richter scale will be unable to record the magnitude. He explains that the smaller quakes (even the last big one in Los Angeles) are trivial compared to what is in store. The super-mega will be preceded by a number of smaller ones, well into the eight-and nine-plus categories.

According to Scallion, when the big one comes, it will remodel the earth's surface and end the world. The big one will not have one epicenter, like most "normal" quakes. Rather, it will be so deep within the earth that the shock waves will come forth in various spots throughout the world, especially along the Pacific Coast from Vancouver, British Columbia, to San Diego, California. Scallion says, "If an 8.0 plus Richter scale quake occurs in the Indian Ocean region—Sri Lanka should be watched carefully [because] within days major earth changes will occur in Japan, Alaska, Italy, Martinique and the Western United States and Canada."

Some psychics believe the reason that the Big One hasn't hit yet is that there are loving vibrations being transmitted from humanity to the soul of the planet. Prophecy collector and author Moira Timms believes that through a heightened awareness to global peace, we've obtained a grace period from the global havoc foreseen by Cayce and other prophets, including Nostradamus and Scallion. New Age prophets who believe the End will come from seismic chaos celebrate the collective consciousness returning to more loving thoughts but wonder if the devastation is canceled or merely delayed. Mirroring some Christian beliefs, including those of the Mormons, who stockpile food and water "just in case," many New Agers believe that one must hope for the best and prepare for the worst.

Paul Solomon, a follower of Cayce and a noted clairvoyant in his own right, believes that the cosmic consciousness of our times changed the outcome of Cayce's predictions. He refers to the breakdown of Soviet tyranny, environmental awareness, etc. He believes that Cayce's prediction of European submersion, perhaps along with the devastation of America, will not come to pass exactly as or when the prophet said. Solomon, however, does believe that we're headed for the End and that we're living on the Eve of Destruction.

A GENTLE CHANGE OF HEART AND MIND

Some New Age prophets believe that rather than a holocaust at the End of the Tribulations, there will be a gentle change of consciousness. Many New Age doomsayers talk about cosmic awareness, spiritual cleansing of the planet, increasing the spiritual vibrations to attune humanity with universal love, alignment of spiritual energies, and various other concepts related to their vision of a postindustrial age of utopia. Ethereal discussions sometimes include such topics as angels, energies, channeled messages and reincarnation, depending on the group involved.

Generally, New Age gurus of Doomsday firmly believe that we can be saved from the Bible's version of Doomsday, with all its miseries, by respecting our fellow Earthlings. In other words, love can save us from the living hell we may have created for ourselves as we approach what seems to be the End.

According to the Reverend Barbra Dillenger, a metaphysical counselor in the San Diego area, "When planet earth reaches a time of dimensional shift and change [the End], it is important to remember that the Universe (which we know as God) never abandons us. One of the ways the Source shares its love is to provide information from knowledgeable intelligences by having [the spiritual energy] born into a body. Another way. . .is by having teachers trance through a loving channel who can be trusted not to misrepresent, alter or misuse this needed support. The tranced information then assists us in understanding and in making personal adjustments with grace and ease."

Lee Carroll is an author and teacher in these changing (or end) times. He believes he has been appointed by the universe to channel the energy of Kryon. Carroll received the news that the world is coming to an end directly from this spiritual messenger. Calling earth a "school," Kryon explained to Carroll that the End will not come as prophesied throughout history, including the terrible termination of all forms of life. The spiritual energy says this prediction has been changed. "You will not be terminated. . . [or] go through horrible wars and planetary upheaval leaving you by the year 2001." Kryon, through Carroll, says that humanity has earned the right to stay in control of its destiny, "well into the first century of the new millennium." This has been accomplished by "raising the vibration of the planet through thought consciousness over the last 60 years." Kryon admits that it was all accomplished as we hovered on the brink of disaster for humanity, one minute before the 12th hour.

Kryon does admit that some people will be terminated and returned to earth with new powers, including the power of telepathic communication. Kryon tells the world that people are about to change and the changes will make life easier for everyone on the planet. Kryon cautions that we must work for peace within our own time or there is a possibility that the End may revert back to the scenario of the other soothsayers of Doomsday. He exhorts: "Dear ones, these are your times. . .take them!"

OR POSSIBLY WE'LL NEED MORE THAN LOVE

Just as Christians do not agree on the exact principles at play during the End Times, New Agers differ too. The spiritual energy of Kryon, mentioned above, assures us that we'll be fine as long as we don't blow it by making war. Lora Adaile Toye, author of the *New World Atlas*, channels End Times information from the spiritual hierarchy of masters, who are part of the Great White Brotherhood, [a group of advanced soul-minds in the ethnic world]. Toye says, "In 1991, the Masters began giving the first geo-energetic explanations for this planet. [The Masters'] interaction with the earth and the transition is one based on service to humankind, designed to enlighten and bring us into a new age of expanded awareness and enlightened thinking, living and being. It is also my belief that the [information on] earth changes was given with much love for humanity, and was never intended to instill fear."

However, Toye does report total earth changes will produce plenty of fear that should be nearly finished by the year 2000. Therefore, the name of her book is prescient in that, should these alterations come to pass, we will indeed need a new world atlas. Toye's channeled spirits outline a new and improved world. She gives specific details as to what will happen to the United States, and it's not a pretty picture. Not only will Scallion's super-mega quake occur, but there will be massive volcanic explosions, causing storms of ash to cloud the skies, and then mammoth rains. The rains will be so intense that they will cause the fault lines to get mushy and slip, which will then cause more earthquakes.

The Masters have informed Toye that there will be no sun for two years, and people will attempt to stay warm by burning wood. This, unfortunately, will only add to the pollution caused by the ashen rains. Moreso, the north and south poles will shift slightly, making tremendous changes in the weather and climate patterns of the world. She also predicts, from the channeled information provided by Saint Germain and other spirits she's been in contact with, that there will be great meteorite storms, even more flooding and towering tidal waves.

But there's more. It has also been predicted here that the Great Lakes will empty into the Mississippi Valley, cutting the country in two and taking away a large part of Texas. (The good news is that there will be safe areas in the mountains of Montana and in the Dakotas.) She has channeled information that says there will be a new Continental Divide in Kansas and that the Rocky Mountains will sink. After the year 2000, the changes that haven't been accomplished will be completed gradually. There are no dates for the final settling, called the Golden Age, but the forming of a new bay in the grassy flatlands of Denver will be a signal that all should be quiet shortly.

Cosmic forces will somehow protect Washington, D.C. Toye channels, "[The Masters] are saying that this area has been of great service to our country, but after the changes, it will no longer be the political center of the country." She reports that people in the future will travel to Washington to view it as a historic landmark, but the new United States will have several political centers.

On the bright side, Toye predicts that after the upheavals she's outlined, there will be a Golden Age of peace, love and concern for all. The world does look rosy after the End, and the engaging thought is that it has many of the same aspects as the Christians' view of life after the Tribulation.

CLOSE ENCOUNTERS OF VARIOUS KINDS

In the movie *Close Encounters of the Third Kind*, we are asked to believe that extraterrestrial beings are here to make contact with the residents of planet Earth. Hollywood didn't think up this concept, of course.

Modern ufology started on June 24, 1947, when Kenneth Arnold reported a flying disk over Washington's Mount Rainier. Arnold said the disk was skipping over the water, and his claims gathered worldwide attention. UFOs have been sighted by tens of thousands since then. Believers run into the millions, and include former president Jimmy Carter. More than fifty percent of Americans, according to a Gallup poll, believe in the possibility of UFOs. Reports come from all social and economic groups and from around the world. The reports are shockingly similar, too.

Scientists, nonetheless, believe that if people understood more about astronomy, UFO reports would drop to nil. They attribute many reports to planets that are especially bright (such as Venus, Jupiter and Mars). Scientists also believe that many sightings are in fact meteors, weather balloons, helicopters, military planes, missile launches, manmade rockets and satellites re-entering the atmosphere, cloud formations, kites, flares, lightning bolts and even birds.

Throughout the years, there have been numerous sightings of unidentified flying objects. Their reality has continued to be hotly debated by scientists, journalists, the government and the general public. However, for some doomsayers, the UFOs are the fulfillment of biblical prophecies warning that "fearful sights and great signs shall there be from heaven," and the sightings reinforce the idea that time is nearly up.

Hal Lindsey, Bob Larson and other Fundamentalist ministers, teachers and believers suggest that UFOs are evidence not of aliens from another planet or galaxy but of demons, and that Satan is at work communicating anti-Christian messages and abducting people. Larson says, "If it can be concluded that the majority of UFOs are of demonic origin, then what is their ultimate purpose? Couldn't the devil just as easily accomplish his ends by another means, or do UFOs serve a unique role in the master plan of Satan to deceive mankind?"

Some Christians judge that the increase in reported UFO sightings in recent years is the devil's way of familiarizing humanity with paranormal activity, so that we will not be scared to death when we see other "miracles," such as fire falling from heaven, the revitalization of the dead and other supernatural feats that they insist can only be attributed to the Antichrist.

David Allen Lewis, a Christian and a UFO buff, writes in a digest devoted to End Times phenomena, "There is no longer any reasonable doubt. . .that the modern UFO manifestations are demonic in origin and activity. . .even though they sometimes have physical manifestation." Lewis believes, like quite a number of

Christians, that UFOs and other intelligences are working to dupe humanity. He says, "UFOs figure into the scheme of End Time prophecy and its fulfillment. It's no accident that the incredible emphasis on alien beings, flying saucers and extraterrestrials, has burst upon humanity in recent times." He concludes that UFOs are part of the devil's master plan to "Prepare the minds of humanity for the [evil] reception."

It does seem likely that if aliens were to appear among us we would believe in their superior intelligence, since their technology would presumably be far beyond our own. They would, in a sense, be miracle workers.

Christians point out that this is exactly what the Bible has prophesied. This isn't some newfangled vision. In Rev. 13:14, John foretells that the miracles to be performed by the Antichrist will be used to hoodwink humanity. "And he deceiveth them that dwell on the earth, by the means of those miracles which he had power to do in the sight of the beast; saying to them that dwell on the earth, that they should make an image to the beast, which had the wound by a sword, and did live."

New Age science author Moira Timms believes that the UFOs have a heroic mission. She writes in her book *Beyond Prophecies and Predictions* that these beings have come from more advanced planets and have been visiting Earth since humanity was merely a spark of potential, a lump of protoplasmal, primordial, atomic globules, sloshing around in a swamp of creativity. She and others believe that the increase in UFO sightings and contacts is due to increased observation on the part of the aliens. "It is of universal, cosmo-geological interest when a leading species, a planet and a solar system are in a crisis and at the same time due to experience some accelerated and drastic evolution," she writes.

Will the aliens rush in like some sort of twenty first-century cavalry to save us in the nick of time? Some ufologists believe this is their intention. Others say they're just taking notes so that they themselves don't commit the same mistakes.

Some New Agers believe that the UFOs are not space people, but spirits, guides, entities and/or angels with a heavenly mission. They are here to assist mortals and give guidance in these difficult times. Others say that the beings who fly the UFOs are willing to help save our planet in this time of great ecological and economic misery. They've been watching us for years.

Some New Agers believe that these aliens built the Egyptian pyramids and have been observing us ever since. Another faction of ufologists say that when the time is right, those who truly believe in space aliens will be swept off the planet. Or perhaps, they will be left and the evildoers will be taken away, and the planet will become a paradise.

In the 1950s, astronomer Donald Menzel presented the theory that the celestial lights mentioned by early philosophers, including Pliny, Seneca and Aristotle, would today be considered UFOs. In ancient times, the lights were called "chasms." They were believed to be breaks in the heavens that allowed celestial light to shine through to earth. Some of the ancient scientists and philosophers believed that the lights anticipated the end of the world. It is, of course, impossible to ascertain what the lights actually were; meteors or supernovas are two possible explanations given by scientists and astronomers. However, many of today's ufologists believe, as the ancients did, that increased reports of UFOs mean our world is headed for change.

Some ufologists believe that the aliens are time travelers coming back to this age from a post-millennium time when humanity has evolved into superintelligent beings who communicate telepathically. Some New Age believers speculate that aliens are living here on the earth but that we do not have the mental capability to see them. Sometimes, however, they slip through a psychic window to visit with us.

The reports of those people who believe they have communicated with extraterrestrial beings tend to exhibit remarkable similarities. Many report that the aliens have large heads, are small in stature and incredibly intelligent, far more so than any earthling. They (or their ships) travel at incredible speeds, and most cannot be photographed.

KaRene, an Arizona-based psychic and channeler of the space being Soltec, announced in 1991 that if we earthlings annihilate ourselves, the aliens have a plan. In a channeled session, KaRene was told: "Should you have a cycle closing out because of nuclear devices, don't you think for one moment that your air would not be filled with craft of all sizes. All of us. . .and I speak for every member of the substation platform. . .are working on an Exodus." They have an escape plan for us.

This plan is known to many New Agers as the World Evacuation Project. At the time humanity truly makes a mess of this planet, UFO contacts and others specially trained by aliens will be swept off the earth before destruction really settles in. This, of course, is much like the Christian concept of Rapture, minus Jesus Christ's intervention.

Those who believe in this World Evacuation Project explain that aliens have been forecasting our destruction for years. The aliens have warned of everything from overpopulation to absolute pollution as our final Armageddon. Some hope that when the End finally does happen, the space folks will come to save us. One theory of New Age ufologists is that some people will be put to sleep to lessen the trauma of the times. They will be kept in a state of inanimation until the earth is cleansed and ready for rehabitation. Some earthlings will remain on the spaceships and live out their lives there. Another group will be taken to special planets to be debriefed about the experience and acclimate themselves before being transported to alien cities. Believers say that the destination, after the End, really depends on the individual, his or her life patterns and individual spiritual evolution.

Baird Wallace, author of *The Space Story and the Inner Light*, says that since the 1950s he and his group have been channeling information regarding human evolution from higher intelligences, called Space Brothers, who are natives of another dimension. Wallace says that the Space Brothers warn of devastation to come.

They have told him that the earth is about to enter into a new "sector" in space that has a different vibrational frequency. The higher vibration rate is affecting every atom of the planet and its inhabitants. The long-term result of this cosmic change, according to Wallace, will be a positive but definite alternation in the state of our consciousness.

Wallace's contacts also warn that we are fast approaching an unseen star. When it enters our solar system, within the next 15 years, life won't be the same, to say the least. It seems that suddenly one morning we'll see another sun, a glowing orange ball. This will be just the tip of the cosmic changes because the Space Brothers have also told him that after the new sun appears, causing climatic changes, skin cancer, crop devastation and other forms of havoc, a new planet will be discovered in our solar system. It is to be called Vulcan and will orbit near Mercury—but not for long, as it will be absorbed by the sun. Then Pluto will be lost (or shot from) the solar system, and finally, the End will come as the planets collide.

In a communication from a Space Brother known as Oxal, reported on October 11, 1975, Wallace was told: "When I mentioned that your solar system is going through a great change, I mean that there are going to be changes in the locations of your planets, stars and satellites. You are going to become a binary sun system, and when this new sun moves into your solar system, the magnetic center of your system will change, and so will the locations of your planets. They will have to readjust to the two suns."

Wallace, in contact with another Space Brother known as Yaum, explains that on one of the final moonwalks, one of the astronauts sighted the new sun, which is still a long way off, but was kept secret in a government cover up. Although it will not become brilliant until it enters our solar system, the sun will cause a shift in the magnetic field and everything that rotates around the magnetic center of the solar system.

The appeal of UFOs, from the perspective of sociologists, may be attributed to escapism. It may stem from the hope that humanity will be saved from itself by a power outside of our human influence. This, as we've seen, is similar to the appeal of the Rapture and the Second Coming. Thus, since things can't get any worse, some supernatural force will come in and save us.

THE END IS IN THE STARS AND NUMBERS

In 1962, Hindu astrologers went on record saying that the End was fast approaching. They based this premise on the alignment of eight planets in Capricorn. This was to be the final curtain call, the Big Day. Millions of believers were driven to panic. Other astrologers saw something different in this fateful year. Some New Age doom-sayers believe that 1962 was the year that the Antichrist was born.

Astrologers have long debated the date for the End. Some now believe that the Age of Aquarius, the supposed two-thousand-year period of enlightenment, joy, peace and closeness to the Universal Love (or God), will be ushered in when the sun arrives in the sign of Aquarius. However, calculations as to exactly when that will happen vary depending on the astrologer. The Hermetic Order of the Golden Dawn, founded in 1888 in London, was once a powerful and popular mystical and occult society. Members calculated that the End would come in 2160.

Astrologer Jeane Dixon, with her daily astrological forecasts read by millions in their morning papers, said in the mid-eighties that a meteor would strike the earth and an earthquake and tidal wave would "befall us as a result of the tremendous impact of this heavenly body in one of our great oceans." In her autobiography, *My Life and Prophecies*, Dixon explains that the meteor will be the beginning of the End. "It may well become known as one of the worst disasters of the 20th century."

Dixon has not issued other End Times prophecies. Some of her followers are waiting to see if she is correct. However, Dixon's predictions have been right many times, including her attempt to warn President Kennedy not to go to Dallas and definitely not to ride in an open car on November 22, 1963.

Terence McKenna, a University of California–Berkeley scholar and a believer in the New Age version of the End thinks that there's something to the date 2012, identified by Jose Arguelles, author of *The Major Factor*. McKenna has designed a computer software program called *Timeswave Zero*. It is based on the ancient Chinese divination method of I Ching. McKenna believes that the I Ching is the "smashed-up remains" of an ancient lunar calendar. Using fractal mathematics and the I Ching in a complex computer formula, McKenna has determined that the End will occur in 2012. At that point, he says, "all cycles come to zero, a dimension emerges that goes off the graph. We are caught in a temporal maelstrom, spinning around the presence of some transdimensional object."

McKenna's program spits forth Doomsday information like other programs calculate what we owe the IRS. He says that life will terminate on December 21, 2012. "This comes precisely at the end of the Mayan calendar, " McKenna says. "For some reason, ancient people had a fixation on this winter solstice 2012."

NEW AGE END TIMES

New Age doomsayers generally believe that through love and understanding we can change our world for the better. Some believe that it will take a global catastrophe, like a series of tremendous earthquakes, to arouse public awareness that the "times they are a changin'." (Generally, most New Agers assert, like Christians, that times will get worse before they get better.) After a period of heightened awareness, the Age of Aquarius and utopian life will emerge.

There are big differences between the Christian view of utopia and the views of New Age. The New Age utopia is the result of human effort, through spiritual understanding, with some assistance from God, spiritual or even space forces. Christians believe that a lasting utopia will only come about through divine effort, as the Bible prophecizes. The time of tranquillity will begin only when it is hailed by the Prince of Peace, referred to in Isa. 9:6. Most New Agers think that peace will come about through a change in cosmic consciousness. Those New Agers who believe that UFOs and/or other speculative entities are among us, or traveling in another dimension, think that we can use the knowledge they have to save ourselves from the End.

Most New Age believers subscribe to the theory that there is no one pathway to God or to the Universal Energy. Most believe in the power of positive thinking and in reincarnation. The notion of a final judgment is not part of their doomsday concept. Virtually all New Agers embrace the theory that good and bad karma provide whatever reward or punishment is needed, rather than damnation, fire and brimstone.

Many Christians are apprehensive of the New Age movement, though liberal Christians accept the fact that there are varied viewpoints. Conservative Christians believe that New Agers are helping along the Antichrist's diabolical cause as they worship the devil and communicate with the dead through sorcery and evil. They believe that the New Age theories are organized by Satan, whose army of demonic soldiers is recruiting more New Age advocates. Some Fundamentalists refer to the New Age movement as the Lucifer Age and exclaim that the New Agers are attempting to destroy Christianity. Less-conservative Christians feel that these alternative spiritually-based groups are misguided, and when being kind, say that their ideas are flawed. They look down on the New Agers and believe that flitting from one New Age ideology to another makes the concept superficial, fraudulent and cultish.

The ideas of Doomsday offered by New Agers and Christians have similarities, although many in each group would hotly deny that fact. Some of the New Age theories are based on traditional Christian beliefs; some of the Christian dogma sounds New Age. It is important to keep in mind that neither group is without imperfections, nor is the dogma unflawed. People are not perfect. All groups have radicals and followers who are too enthusiastic to see anyone else's point of view. And in studying Doomsday, it may be wise to look at a diverse collection of ideas specifically addressing what humanity is doing, could do or is not doing to save the planet from certain death.

NEW AGE THEORIES, FUMBLES AND QUESTIONABLE ENDS

Did you know we were recently saved from Doomsday? A prayer battery saved the West Coast. It was designed from plans shared through UFO contact, and we can thank George King and the Aetherius Society. Founded in 1955 in London, the society is a New Age group and one of the more popular UFO sects. In the 1950s, the group's founder, George King, began to psychically channel information from the Aetherius Masters, a highly evolved group of soul-minds. It was provided to King, as a human contact, in order to save the world from imminent doom.

Gaining recognition, King moved to California and gathered more followers. (He now has headquarters in Los Angeles, Detroit and London.) King and his devotees are connected with the voices, they assert. The transmissions, recorded for future generations, are said to come from space, and sometimes from Venus. King says, "In years to come, these tapes will be an impeachable [sic] reference source as to the exact words of the cosmic masters," including the master Jesus.

The masters told King to work, serve their mission and attempt to save the earth. In one such attempt, called Operation Blue Water, King and his followers built a glass pyramid filled with coils and maneuvered in a boat over the "psychic center" of the earth. King had forecast a massive earthquake that would destroy California, marking the beginning of the End. Through the TAS's work and the machine, the earthquake supposedly was prevented. King says, "The fact that the West Coast of America is still intact proves [the operation's] success."

TAS continued to "serve humanity" and defuse the Doomsday time bomb. One of its methods was the construction by King of a device known as a "prayer battery." The mechanism, hidden inside a large blue box, is "capable of receiving the highest frequencies of spiritual energies and putting them in a psychic container," King says. Followers load the box on Thursday evenings in a "charging session," and the prayer leader begins preaching. The prayers are graded on a subject scale by the congregation. Good prayers (devoutly intense) add to the battery; poor ones detract. The battery stores up the good ones and the power of the prayers is let loose in times of famine, earthquakes, wars and other crises, or prior to a forthcoming catastrophic event (like the Pacific earthquake mentioned above), in order to prevent it.

At one time, followers guarded the secrets of the TAS with the utmost care. This was especially true of the prayer battery (constructed to save the world) which they said they'd defend with their lives. They believed that the "evil power" of the Soviet Union would go to any lengths to obtain its secrets.

While the TAS predicts the end of the world, TAS followers believe they can delay or change destiny through the use of the prayer battery. Even though they are assisting nonbelievers and humanity in general to avoid the end until everyone has converted to the society, they are also anxious for D day to hit. Doomsday is the "blessed hope" of this sect.

Get ready, because the poles are about to shift. In theory, the rotation of the earth is about to change, making it wobble from its axis and then flip. If it only shifts 90 degrees, Santa will have to call Hawaii or North Africa home. At 180 degrees, he'll be wishing kids "Merry Christmas" with a southern accent. In reality, should this occur, all of life would be destroyed. Those who predict a shift in the poles believe such an event would fulfill certain Bible prophecies, as well as those of Nostradamus and Edgar Cayce.

People who believe that the poles are about to shift, commonly known as pole shifters, see this as the ultimate disaster. It will cause enormous tidal waves as oceans become displaced from their basins. Hurricane winds of unrecorded velocity will rip around the planet and earthquakes will completely reshape the continents. Volcanoes will spit lava high into the heavens as they vomit poisonous gases that will exterminate any life form that happens to escape the other catastrophes.

Should the poles shift less than 180 degrees, the icecaps would melt and re-form in another spot and the sea levels would rise, washing away a goodly part of the planet's civilization. John White, author of *Pole Shift*, writes, "Climates will change instantly, and the geography of the globe will be radically altered. . .large numbers of organisms, including the human race, will be decimated or even become extinct."

In 1982, pole-shift expert Peter Warlow presented his theories in a paper, *Reversing Earth*. In it, he claimed that an extraterrestrial source will trigger the pole shift. He believes that it is possible for a celestial body to exert a torque on the earth even though it does not come into direct contact. Warlow writes, "We, thus, have the means of turning the earth over. . . ." However, he insists, "There is nothing special about the year 2000." He believes that the shift could happen in days, weeks, months or thousands of years from today.

Pole shifters predicted that unprecedented seismic activity would occur between 1982 and 1984 as a result of the "Jupiter effect"—the gravitational pull created by the planets' lining up on the opposite side of the sun from the earth. Their gravitational pull on the earth would be sufficient, supposedly, to produce a humongous earthquake—big enough to give Arizona beachfront property. Quake jokes aside, the effects were to be devastating. (Hal Lindsey and other Bible scholars were among those who bought into this theory.) Many pole shifters believed that the final tick on the doomsday clock was about to be heard.

Paul Solomon, a noted psychic, believed that the Jupiter effect would quite possibly be the end to life. He believed that Japan would disappear beneath the sea, the Great Lakes would empty into the Gulf of Mexico, new continents would spring up from the Atlantic and Pacific oceans; [Most of the Pacific Coast (lower Washington State to California) would sink. He predicted that the Jupiter effect, which would occur before the pole shifted, would also split the continental United States in two.

Another pole-shifting prophet, Aron Abrahamsen, said that by 1981, unless people stopped fighting and began to love one another again, the poles would surely shift. Like numerous other New Age pole shifters, Abrahamsen believed that love and peace represented our only hope of preventing the shift.

Various other prophets believe the eruption of Mount St. Helens and the terrible earthquakes in California are the telltale signs of shifting.

More than ten years after the release of his book, pole-shift expert John White now says that the situations that served as the basis for his predictions have changed. "On the basis of a decade's hindsight," he now writes, "I think that the possibility of a catastrophic pole shift at the end of this century is highly unlikely. To be more precise *I do not think a pole shift will occur as predicted.*" However, like other prophets of Doomsday, he continues to hedge his bets. He says we must switch our thoughts to God and answer the question: Are we ready to die?

Active in the 1960s, the Light Affiliates, headquartered in Burnaby, British Columbia, became media makers when they issued the following statement:

> We wish to notify all those interested that a phenomenon has occurred here in Vancouver. A young girl, age 22, suddenly began channeling on October 23, 1969. Her source is a being identifying himself as Ox-Ho, who is relaying transmissions from a galaxy close to our own. . . .Her material is phenomenal in that she has been informed of the coming disasters, when to expect them, and what to do pertaining to the necessary evacuation of the danger areas and food supplies, etc., that will be needed.

This contemporary prophet of doom was Robin McPherson, renamed "Estelle" by the alien informant or contact. Others in the group were also renamed by the spokes-alien, but it was never clear why this was necessary. However, the foreigner to earth did say that the final days would begin on November 22, 1969. He told Estelle that in these final hours, man would be "given one last opportunity to repair his decadent house before the terminal series of disasters." And if we didn't spit-polish the planet? "Space Brothers would remove the Chosen and return them to Earth after the planet has once again been 'crystallized,' and been spiritually, as well as physically, restructured." The Light Affiliates explained that the restructuring meant a shift in the magnetic poles.

When the date of the End came and went and the Light Affiliates were still on earth, Estelle's transmitted messages stopped. Her mother, who changed her name and is now known as Magdalene, took up the task. In the mid-1970s when she was asked by a journalist how the Space Brothers could have been wrong, Magdalene replied, "We misinterpreted them. . .because it all happened so suddenly. The first visions I was given of destruction were very upsetting. I can see things now in a much broader perspective. . .The thing is that it is the first ascension, and it is a *mental* ascension. The Brothers are trying to get as many people as possible into the Kingdom. . .You know, I've been told by the Brotherhood that earth is like an encounter therapy center for the psychotics of the universe. . .I have been shown that the earth is also wobbling very drastically on its axis."

Like other cults and Doomsday groups when the appointed time of destruction came and went, the Light Affiliates reorganized but the movement slowly lost its plausibility. Interestingly enough, it often takes several disconfirmations to destroy the credibility or the purpose of such groups.

In the next chapter, we'll look at Doomsday from a global perspective and discuss the impact of our history and lifestyle on the environment. Will the population explosion actually be the cause of the End? What do environmentalists have to say about all the gook that's killing the trees, the streams, the oceans and the air? Let's find out.

The fear—and more often the hope—
that the world will come to a quick and violent end is. . .
very much with us today.
—DANIEL COHEN, *WAITING FOR THE APOCALYPSE*

8
ENVIRONMENTAL IMPACT

Theories on the End are not confined to hallowed religious quarters or New Age channelers. They are everyday issues, on the minds of many.

Vine Victor Deloria, Jr., a Standing Rock Sioux, an author and an environmentalist, wrote:

> Religion can be kept within the bounds of sermons and scriptures. It is a force in itself and it calls for the integration of lands and peoples in harmonious unity. The lands [of the planet] wait for those who can discern their rhythms. The particular genius of each continent, each river valley, the rugged mountains, the placid lakes, all call for relief from the constant burden of exploitation.

More recently, the fervent environmentalist and current vice president Al Gore wrote in his book *Earth in the Balance*, "Our ecological system is crumbling as it suffers a powerful collision with the hard surfaces of a civilization speeding out of control. The damage is remarkably sudden and extensive in the context of the long period of stability in the environment before the damage, but we see the destruction in slow motion." He continues with the grim picture of an ecological Doomsday and says, "It is as if the force of its collision with nature has pushed it abruptly backward in a crushing blow, like a dashboard striking the forehead of a child."

Many in the global community of secular and scientific groups nod their heads in agreement at Gore's words. They firmly believe that we're headed for the great big D (as in Doomsday). And when it happens, they know whose fault it will be. Any guesses? That's right. Ours. We have been abusing our planet, they say. We haven't been sufficiently careful with this precious planet.

Even those folks who do not believe in the Bible's version of the Second Coming, the theories of Nostradamus or UFOs wonder if we'll eventually be annihilated because of a massive wave of unprocessed sludge or disgusting gobs of sewage taking over the world. Or will we destroy the rain forests of the entire planet, thus curtailing oxygen production so we're unable to breathe? Will the climatic changes seen in the last few years slow production of food and cause global famine? What of plagues and overpopulation? Or will we come to our end as did the dinosaurs?

Anne H. Ehrlich and Paul R. Ehrlich, ecologists and authors, write that many believe that science can pull a technological rabbit out of the hat to solve any ecological problem. "They don't understand that there are very important laws of nature that limit what kinds of rabbits can be pulled out of which hats, and so persist in assuming, among other things, that perpetual motion machines will soon be with us." Some of those rabbits, the authors explain, are sprinkling our planet with noxious droppings, so we would be better off if they had never left the hat in the first place.

THE END AND THE ENVIRONMENTALISTS

Science and religion often seem at odds with each other, yet many environmentalists agree with the Fundamentalists who say that the End is approaching and it's not a pretty sight. The environmentalists' mode of destruction sometimes even sounds like it comes straight from the Book of Revelation.

In *Our Angry Earth*, Isaac Asimov, best-selling author and commentator on scores of scientific subjects, says that, contrary to what some Christians believe, "It is not adultery and fornication that is threatening humanity, but physical pollution. It is not an angry god who is threatening to destroy everything; it is a poisoned planet—poisoned by us."

Frederik Pohl, a well-known speaker on global issues, and the co-author of *Our Angry Earth*, tells us we've already gone too far to stop the hands of the Doomsday clock. However, he believes we can slow the process. "The only choice left to us is to decide how much worse we are willing to let things get."

Despite their gloomy outlook, Asimov and Pohl have designed a plan called Techno-Cures. Their solutions range from conservation of fossil fuels to changes in living and eating habits. They believe that solving or slowing our environmental woes will require large-scale alterations in our lifestyles, and they admit that industry will be damaged and businesses will be harmed. They admit that some people will find the changes unpleasant. The authors say, "The reason for this isn't that do-gooder environmentalists like ourselves insist on it because of some idealistic devotion to 'nature' or the spotted owl. It's because our profligate ways have done so much harm that large-scale change is inevitable." They say that if we don't clean up our act, the planet will make the choice for us, possibly doing away with humanity in the process.

A good number of scientists concur that there is considerable merit to the notion that we're in quicksand up to our armpits and that environmental problems are ready to suck us under. However, many think that the circumstances aren't as dire as we are being led to believe by the media and environmental lobbies. This backlash is typically headed by conservative academics and columnists. Another group says that environmental scientists have deliberately slanted data to win their causes. Some of the gloomy warnings that are flashed across the screen of our television sets are questionable, even when they are based on a bit of truth. But scientists, as well as our own common sense, say that it is reckless to dismiss the question of an environmental Doomsday. We know that we're in the middle of some pretty terrible goop and muck when entire cities are warned not to drink the tap water. Or when countless children living in the same neighborhood are stricken by cancer. However, one must attempt to look carefully at the theory of End Times.

ANIMAL EXTINCTION AND THE END

"You can tell the End is coming because species are becoming extinct," numerous environmentalists have insisted since the late 1970s, when biologists identified a correlation between dwindling numbers of falcons and tigers and the health and cleanliness of the earth. In 1979, biologist Norman Myers, heading a worldwide field study of only one animal a year, told the press that according to his theories there would be a loss of over 1 million different species by the year 2000. One million birds, reptiles and mammals would not only be endangered, but gone except to be seen in movies and encyclopedias and as stuffed replicas in museums. Myers based this theory on his own calculations, calling this alarming statistic a "reasonable working figure."

As was expected, the public was up in arms, scared to death of that prophecy because it meant that eventually people would become extinct, too. While the public was still coming to grips with this terrible statistic, Harvard biologist Edward O. Wilson claimed that it was far too conservative. Actually, we were losing 4,000, or 30,000, or 50,000 species per year (Wilson has used all three figures at various times).

Wilson based his theory on a mathematical equation called the species-area cure. It related the size of an island to the number of species found on it. According to the hypothesis, if the island is 10 square miles, it will typically have half as many types of animals as an island of 100 square miles. Applying his principle, if 2 percent of all rain forests are leveled in a year, 50,000 species will be lost.

Critics say that it ain't necessarily so, and that a sweeping generalization about the planet cannot be made using this formula, since species are able to adapt in various ways. And what's found to be true on an island often isn't the case when applied to a large forest area. Recently Brazilian zoologists searched the forests attempting to confirm the extinction theory. They couldn't confirm a single case and actually "rediscovered" some animals thought to have died out over twenty years ago. Despite extensive inquiries from environmental lobbies, Vernon Heywood, former chief scientist with the International Union for the Conservation of Nature and Natural Resources, which works with governments to protect truly endangered animals, said that the organization does not have "sufficient evidence to support the conclusion that massive extinctions have taken place within the last 20 years."

Though many scientists are pushing for practical conservation measures to protect animals and the loss of their habitats, environmentalists often use questionable data in order to draw attention to very pressing concerns. While the members of the animal kingdom may not be dying at the rate of 50,000 species a year, there have been changes, and the public does have a right to know. Heywood and other scientists believe that we must address the issue of where and how environmental Doomsday claims originate before making decisions on public policy.

OVERPOPULATION AND THE END

Environmental doomsayers believe that unless the world population is checked, by the year 2050 it will have doubled, stretching resources well beyond the breaking point.

In the mid-nineties, China had the largest population of any country in the world, with nearly 1.2 billion people. India had 912 million people. The United States came in third with 261 million, followed by Indonesia (200 million people) and Brazil (with 155 million people).

The United Nations is concerned about the population boom, as are many countries, including the United States. Each year the world population has shown a growth of about 90 million people. (About 141 million babies are born per year; about 51 million deaths occur each year worldwide.) Every minute the population grows by 170 people. The reason for concern is that with overpopulation come shortages of basic necessities, specifically quality air, water and food.

Bruce Alberts, president of the National Academy of Sciences says, "Science and technology can do a lot of things, but what they cannot do is make finite resources support an infinite population." Henry Kendall, Nobel Prize winner and member of the Union for Concerned Scientists, says, "If we do not stabilize population with justice, humanity and mercy. . .it will be done for us by nature, and it will be done brutally."

Al Gore has said, "We are now adding the equivalent of one China's worth of people every 10 years, one Mexico's worth of people every single year. Societies cannot maintain stability with that kind of. . .growth."

In 1994, for the first time in decades, environmentalists, scientists and population experts came together under the auspices of the United Nations in a serious effort to deal with the problem of overpopulation. The International Conference on Population and Development adopted a lengthy plan that sets ambitious goals to control population. The plan addresses universal access to family planning, equal educational opportunities for women, lower infant mortality rates and higher economic and educational status for women in developing countries. It also recommends that governments take steps to reduce deaths from unsafe abortions, discourage reliance on abortion and provide treatment for complications due to abortion. The plan supports abortion as a woman's reproductive right in countries where it is illegal. The goal of the conference was to find a way to keep the world population from rising above 7.8 billion by 2050, up from 5.6 billion today.

Bisi Ogunleye, president of a Nigerian women's association and a delegate at the conference said, "Those who are rich, it is time for you to share your riches. . .if you don't, the poor will share their poverty." Without some check on population, conference delegates fear that there will be endemic poverty and mass starvation.

According to environmentalists, global family planning and the fears of drastic overpopulation were greatly downplayed by the Reagan and Bush administrations. Both presidents are blamed for not addressing this pressing issue.

Family planning since the sixties has achieved a measure of success. The United Nation reports that the average number of children born to a woman in a developing country has dropped from 6 to 4. In the United States, the average woman has 2.1 children; in Spain, the figure is 1.2; in Japan, it's 1.5 and in Germany, 1.3. In the United States, the number of married women using any method of contraceptive has risen from a meager 10 percent to over half. And the annual population growth has actually dropped from 2.1 percent to 1.6 percent, but environmentalists say that's not enough. Even nations formerly against family planning are taking a second look at the population explosion, including Islamic countries and Catholic countries such as Peru.

Even though family planning is seen as the way to slow this Doomsday threat, it has provoked fiery opposition. Catholic leaders strongly oppose the plan outlined by the conference because it doesn't prevent the use of abortion and endorses birth control for all women, married and unmarried. (The Vatican officially opposes the use of abortion and "unnatural" family planning, i.e., any use of condoms, contraceptives or sterilization.) The Vatican is attempting to sway family-planning advocates; the Pope is lobbying world leaders to stop the global program, based on the Church's opposition to contraceptives and abortion. Pope John Paul II says the world political leaders are overstepping their ethical bonds by encouraging abortion and artificial contraception. The Pope's opinion will not be changed by a world conference even though the Vatican sees overpopulation as "serious and grave."

Paul and Anne Ehrlich, co-authors of *The Population Explosion*, have been spreading dire predictions about overpopulation and the End since the mid-seventies. Their most optimistic scenario ended with the death of only half a billion people in a major "die-back" by 1985. Like other soothsayers, even when that did not come to pass, they didn't stop waxing prophetic about how we'll starve.

The Ehrlichs warn: "One thing seems safe to predict: starvation and epidemic disease will raise death rates over most of the planet." They have predicted massive famines, ecological disasters, nuclear wars and raging epidemics.

The world has always seen massive famines, most recently in Africa, but nothing like what Ehrlich has predicted. The world has yet to experience a "die-back" in its human population, yet the Ehrlich's theories are still widely applauded.

Hunger is an everyday threat to millions of human beings throughout the world. The Washington, D.C.–based environmental group Worldwatch Institute says food production reached its maximum potential in the 1980s. Now it's downhill. Because of overproduction, even high-tech agriculture cannot keep up with the usurping of soil, erosion and lack of water. And, ultimately, the human species will perish.

Worldwatch predicts D-day consequences that sound like they're right out of the New Testament, which says that, "in various places there will be famines" (Matt. 24:7). In the Book of Rev. 6:8, we read, "And I looked and behold, an ashen horse; and he who sat on it had the name Death; and Hades was following with him. And authority was given to them over the fourth of the earth, to kill with sword and with famine and with pestilence and by the wild beasts of the earth."

Worldwatch predicts an ugly, desolate future. With momentous weather changes occurring, causing everything from midwestern floods nearly every year to extensive drought through the world, food production is slipping to a dangerously low level. George Borgstrom, author of *Hungry Planet*, cautions that no part of the world except the United States is more than one year away from starvation should production of food cease because of a critical crop failure. However, Americans should not gloat, because Borgstrom says the U.S. is only two years away from massive starvation under similar circumstances.

According to the eminent agricultural scientist Dr. Norman Borlaug, an expert on world food production, it is foolhardy to think we can solve the slowdown in food production and the question of overpopulation satisfactorily. Dr. Borlaug has been called "the father of the Green Revolution" because of his knowledge of high-tech agriculture, yet he believes that the doom and gloom are valid. He contends that it's folly to expect science to solve the food production problem in the eleventh hour. He says that he believes the anticipated "hunger and misery of millions would provoke a great global holocaust." Sociologists now tell us, too, that there's a direct correlation between hunger and increased violence.

THE MOWING DOWN OF THE RAIN FOREST

Doomsayers bring worldwide attention to the devastation of the tropical rain forests. Al Gore says in *Earth in the Balance*, "At the current rate of deforestation, virtually all the tropical rain forests will be gone partway through the next century. If we allow this destruction to take place, the world will lose the richest storehouse of genetic information on the planet, and along with it possible cures for many of the diseases that affect us."

The destruction of the rain forest is a favorite issue among D-day environmentalists. They explain that with the obliteration of the rain forest, so goes the flora and fauna and the ability of the plants to filter our air and produce oxygen.

Yet, there is controversy. The theory that a football-field-size chunk of rain forest was being destroyed every second (or 40 million acres a year) originated with a Brazilian scientist who used sensors from a weather satellite to count the number of fires burning in the Amazon. He estimated the size of the fires and theorized that 40 percent were being ignited to clear land. Then his assumption was applied to other rain forests and Gore used these figures to support the Biodiversity Treaty and other initiatives generated to safeguard the environment. But when two American scientists compared weather satellite photos taken in 1978 to others taken in 1988, they found the loss to be only about one fifth of the original figure. This data, however, didn't sketch doom and gloom and barely made the news.

Compton Tucker, of the National Aeronautics and Space Administration, and David Skole, an ecologist at the University of New Hampshire, who performed the research study, found that it was the pattern of cutting that seemed to have the greatest negative effect on the rain forests. They call this the "edge effect" theory. According to the edge-effect equation, many small clearings that are cut into a forest produce more drastic changes than one large clearing of equal size. Wind, poachers and other elements are able to pierce the dense forest when there are many edges to attack and thus compromise the balance of nature and the health of plants and animals. Yes, they believe the rain forests are still in jeopardy, but they may be safer than we originally believed.

THE END AND OZONE HOLES

The gaping hole in the ozone layer is another favorite topic of environmental doomsayers. Some cite increased skin cancer, sheep in South America being blinded by the bright ultraviolet rays and global warming as intense rays of sunlight penetrate the earth's protective ozone layer.

How do the holes we've all heard about happen, and why are they of importance to doomsayers? The holes are caused by man-made chemicals invading the stratosphere. They are called chlorofluorocarbons (CFCs), and as a gas, they are lighter than air, so they rise. When they reach the stratosphere, they break down, and the chlorine molecule is released. This harmless little molecule, however, isn't benign when it comes in contact with the ozone molecules. It turns into a Pac-Man clone and attacks. Its target is the shield we humans need to protect us from those damaging ultraviolet rays that the sun produces.

Loudly speaking out about ozone destruction are groups of environmentalists. A counterattack has been headed by the former Atomic Energy Commission chairperson Dixy Lee Ray, who has written a book called *Trashing the Planet*. Ray claims that any destruction of the delicate layer is due to natural conditions, such as volcanic eruptions and the chemical process generated by sea mist and salt. It is not due to any chemical produced by humans and their machines. This counterattack was dismissed, however, when measurements taken after the great volcanic eruption of Mount Pinatubo in the Philippines indicated no additional increase in the amount of chlorine in the atmosphere. (Ray's claim indicates that there should have been more.) Scientists say *most* volcanic eruptions do not contribute to ozone depletion, with the exception of Mount St. Augustine, which sent about 175,000 tons of chlorine into the stratosphere. (Humanity contributes about 750,000 tons *each year*.)

Scientists report that while chlorine from natural sources, such as volcanoes and salt spray, does go into the atmosphere, as supposed, it never reaches the stratosphere. Instead, it is washed out of the air by rain and returns to earth. However, CFCs aren't like their natural cousin, because they resist the breakdown that neutralizes the natural chlorine. The lowly little ocean plant, plankton, however, does generate methylchloride that makes it up to our delicate stratosphere, yet the contribution is insignificant because it is natural and breaks down.

Middle-of-the-road environmentalists, who are not screaming Doomsday and not pointing fingers at their opponents, say that the claims of ozone depletion are exaggerated. However, many scientists believe the world must speed up the agreed-to international phaseout of CFCs. The United States has to halt the use of CFCs by 1996, but production in China, India and Brazil will not be ceased until 2006. All three countries, becoming more industrialized by the day, are major contributors to the CFC crisis.

Every winter the Antarctic gets extremely cold. The cold intensifies the ozone-munching activity of the chlorine molecule as it eats a hole through the ozone. That's why there is a hole in the atmosphere above the South Pole. If the ozone hole is a reality, why isn't there a hole at the North Pole? The reason sounds quite simple: Moving air is warmer than stagnant air. The Arctic winter is actually warmer than its southern counterpart because of the wind patterns generated by the Arctic mountains. This wind theory is supposedly the reason no hole has been discovered in the Northern Hemisphere. However, this doesn't mean that someday one won't appear because of the use of CFCs, and that's what burns the beef among environmental groups. It has been predicted that it will occur at any moment, and this type of D-day soothsaying makes news. The environmentalists visualize a future of scorching rays, sizzled crops and animals and the ruin of humanity.

Harvard scientist Jim Anderson, one of a group of NASA-funded researchers, says, "It's very poor science to assume that ozone is dropping based on circumstantial evidence of increased chlorine." He and other researchers believe that those who say there is no cause-and-effect link in the Northern Hemisphere are correct. Anderson, who has taken measurements of the chlorine at the South Pole, explains that there is a connection between elevated chlorine there and the depleted ozone but that the holes are not new.

Since the mid-1970s, scientists have reported holes in the ozone (although some environmentalists say the first report was in

1985). In reality the holes may have been there before and simply not tracked as thoroughly or with the sophisticated equipment available today.

What we do not know, and may not know until it's too late, is whether the stratosphere can somehow absorb both natural and man-made CFCs. We know that the stratosphere does cleanse itself naturally. The question is, can it do so quickly enough to keep us from the End?

THE END AND THIS CRAZY WEATHER

Some environmentalists believe that strange new weather patterns will bring on the End. *Time* magazine has called it the "weird weather phenomenon."

El Niño is a huge pool of warm seawater in the western Pacific that expands eastward every few years toward Ecuador. As it moves, it nudges the ocean's jet stream of warm water slightly off course. El Niño has occurred before. However, it normally only lasts from 12 to 18 months. The current El Niño has been with us since the mid-1980s. This change in the temperature of the ocean has produced headline-making weather. There have been record numbers of hurricanes in Hawaii, tornadoes in the southwestern U.S., severe rain throughout the United States, droughts in Africa and floods with subsequent mud slides in California, already on shaky ground after earthquakes and wildfires that compromised mountainsides.

This El Niño is unusual even for El Niños. Oceanographers wonder if maybe it's not just an El Niño, but is really signaling that two or three years ago we had a relatively persistent change in climate. Another weather expert, Gerald Bell, a meteorologist with the National Oceanic and Atmosphere Administration, explains that our current El Niño should have been over years ago; this is the longest one ever on record. From the experts' point of view, there's nothing obvious on which to base this change and no one is sure what is happening.

Some environmentalists insist that the changes in weather are a result of global warming, but few scientists are ready to announce that conclusion. Global warming is the theory that the buildup of CO_2, methane and other heat-trapping gases can raise global temperatures, just as the temperatures are increased in a glass greenhouse. Computer models and complex mathematical formulas support the global-warming theory, however scientists are more cautious. Proponents of the global-warming concept believe that it may be our D-day downfall. They claim the average global temperature has risen over the past century.

More than 20 years ago, Dr. Howard A. Wilcox, a marine scientist, physicist and author of *Hothouse Earth*, began warning that global warming was a bigger threat than a global war, pollution or destruction of the rain forests. He says, "Within the lifetime of our great grandchildren, the oceans may rise, swallowing cities and flooding coasts. New York, Tokyo and London may be destroyed, and the survivors may well be clamoring or warring for space on higher ground" when the polar icecaps melt. He predicts that this will happen sometime in or about the year 2050.

Other environmentalists, including Asimov, chime in and explain that with the melting of the polar icecaps (now about two miles thick at various spots), various American locations will be at considerable risk. They specifically suggest that the coastlines of Florida and Manhattan may need to build Dutch-style dikes to hold the waters back.

Worldwide, in low-lying countries the situation is even more serious. Bangladesh, one of the poorest countries in the world, is located on unstable deltas. Even in "good" years, the monsoons and floods kill and destroy. For instance, in 1970 and again in 1985, a storm surged up from the Bay of Bengal and seawater flooded most of the country, killing millions. Of the 110 million people living in Bangladesh, about 80 million live in threatened areas. An increase in sea level, even just a few inches of water, could displace thousands of people. In Taiwan, on the Vilan plain (one of the country's most productive farming areas), rising levels have already been experienced. The dikes have already been built to keep the rising level of seawater out.

Environmentalists say this story could be repeated throughout the world, from South America's Guyana to the hundreds of coral islands of the South Pacific. It seems that these islands are at particular risk from global warming and the melting of the polar icecaps, since warm water stops the generation of coral, and the structure of the islands is undermined. Without that structure, the islands will sink.

Another major concern regarding the End and the warming of the earth is that as the temperatures heat up, climate zones will move further from the equator toward the poles. This will change the weather and agriculture patterns of the world. Specifically, summers will become more intense, and the Midwest, the "breadbasket of the world," will turn to jungle rather than golden waves of grain.

People and animals can migrate away from the flooded areas and start a new life on higher ground, but trees (our natural filtering and oxygen-generating system) can't pick up roots and move. Changes in climate means certain death for the flora of various parts of the planet. Entire forests could perish. This means less clean air for you and me, for our kids and grandchildren. This type of change has happened in the past, as recorded by fossilized plants and animals, but the old-time records don't indicate what could happen, say the environmentalists, with global warming, uncontrolled deforestation, acid rain, rising sea levels, burning of fossil fuels, warming of the frozen tundra (which currently stores great amounts of carbon dioxide that would be released as it warmed) and pollution that won't quit. Some believe that once real global warming begins to take hold, nothing will stop it. It will self-generate and not stop until there isn't enough free carbon and oxygen in the world to support any life. Asimov writes, "If man does not use this century and the next to develop a no-growth lifestyle, the final and unavoidable hothouse catastrophe will terminate man's present civilization."

It is important to realize, however, that naturally caused warming and cooling cycles are always happening to the earth, and critics of global-warming theories say that the hotter temperatures of the past few years may actually be part of a natural cycle. However, scientists who do not agree with the global warming camp are mixed on the theory of natural climate change. Some assert that we're actually in a cooling trend.

THE END AND COSMIC COLLISIONS

Even patching the hole in the ozone won't help us if those who believe we're headed for a cosmic collision are correct. End-of-the-world predictions of cosmic collisions aren't new. Humanity has been plagued with the fear that the planets could crash for centuries. Some groups currently believe that since the galaxy was started with a big bang, perhaps that's how we'll end, too.

Just since 1970, there have been plenty of near misses as comets and asteroids have passed by our planet. On August 10, 1972, for example, a fireball about the size of a house sailed over Grand Teton National Park. If there had been a fractional change in the orbit, it might have crashed to earth in San Francisco, Portland or Seattle, with an explosive force five times that of the bomb that decimated Hiroshima. On March 23, 1989, the *New York Times* reported that a half-mile wide asteroid swooped through earth's orbit. *Nobody saw it coming.* A team of American scientists who convened a few months later noted that had the asteroid struck the earth, it would have caused an unprecedented disaster.

In 1994, the comet known as Schumaker-Levy 9 crashed into and scarred the planet Jupiter. Could the same thing happen to earth? You bet, say scientists.

The ultra-orthodox Lubavitch interpret the Zohar, an ancient Jewish mystical text, to mean that the End will come when there is an impact on Jupiter. That impact occurred in the summer of '94. The Lubavitch insist that this event foretells the coming of the Messiah.

Other religious groups agree that there will be signs from the heavens when the King of kings is about to return. According to a Gallup survey, sixty-five percent of Americans believe that Jesus will return to earth in an apocalyptic Armageddon. Radio commentator Harold Camping, owner of the Family Radio, in Oakland, California, with a program broadcast to over 40 stations nationwide, tells radio listeners that if you want End Times prophecy fulfillment, it's here. The comet proves it. Camping interpreted the Bible to say that on September 6 or 7, "there will be signs in the sun, moon or stars of such a character that everyone in the world will know that something dreadful is about to happen." And before the end of September 1994, Jesus would return. Unfortunately for Camping and followers, Jesus did not arrive as they'd expected.

From a sociological, scientific and theological perspective, predictions from doomsayers like Camping coming after an astronomical event are not unusual. Roger Williams, a Bible scholar and professor at the University of Michigan, says that the ability to pinpoint the End to the day is generally doubted by people of science or the clergy. Rabbi David Wolpe, of the University of Judaism in Los Angeles, says, "At the end of every century, there is an outpouring of predictions, and a desire to create pattern and meaning out of events. The bigger the event [like the media and print coverage of the comet hitting Jupiter], the more profound."

The public's consternation regarding a fellow planet's little accident is well-founded. An estimated two thousand asteroids wider than 1 kilometer follow orbits that cross the earth's. A collision could have the destructive power of 10,000 megatons of TNT. Such an impact would produce widespread disruption, not only from the loss of life but from the amount of dust it would send into the atmosphere. That alone could, according to scientists, totally alter our weather patterns, triggering widespread crop failure and subsequent universal starvation. Depending on the size of the asteroid, it just might create Doomsday.

According to Clark R. Chapman of the Planetary Science Institute in Tucson and David Morrison of NASA's Ames Research Center in Mountain View, California, authors of *Cosmic Catastrophies,* there is a one-in-ten-thousand chance that a two-kilometer-wide asteroid will hit our planet within the next century. Collisions with larger objects, like the comet that hit Jupiter, will occur much less frequently. Some scientists believe that the last hit from a good-sized asteroid wiped out the dinosaurs and other life forms over 65 million years ago.

What's a planet to do? NASA has proposed an early warning system using sensitive electronic detectors and telescopes. Positioned around the globe, they could detect objects that are threatening the earth.

Morrison and Chapman explain that the peril from small asteroids "is much less than the hazard of other natural catastrophes that can and do kill just as many people much more often." They say that it would be nearly impossible to discover and inventory all of the countless objects that could possibly hit us. And conservative taxpayers are likely to agree that the expense of building and maintaining expensive surveillance equipment and the danger posed by explosive devices (used to destroy incoming asteroids) may be out of proportion to the actual threat.

Chapman and Morrison say that an individual's risk of being a target for an asteroid—whether or not he or she is actually killed—is about the same as accidentally being electrocuted, or about 1 in 300,000 per year.

If the odds are this high, why are there so few reports of people being smashed by asteroids? Astronomers tell us that the risk figures are correct—it's just that if the rocks hit, a lot of us will go together. Most believe that since the odds are actually in our favor, we can wait for a short time and come up with a plan and new technology, perhaps costing less, to warn of cosmic threats and avert asteroids headed at us.

Chapman and Morrison say that ignoring this threat, nonetheless, is irrational. They support a Doomsday deflection plan. "If nothing is discovered to be on a collision course, we have lost nothing. If instead, a doomsday impact is discovered and averted, then we will have made one of the most important contributions to human civilization in history." Many astronomers believe that it would be wise to practice the diversion plan on a few distant asteroids before the big one approaches. This would be done to just make sure it works and that all systems are go.

On a shade happier note regarding cosmic Doomsday, some astronomers believe that we are on a collision course with galaxy M31, known as the Andromeda galaxy. The collision with M31 is however, a very long way off, and even if the collision tears our galaxy apart and causes our sun to go shooting off on a career of its own, the planets in our solar system will be safe—that is, we're safe, too. The planets are so tightly bound that they'd just go along for the ride. Astronomers tell us that, yes, we'd see a whole lot of new-to-us stars, but that would be the only significant effect.

However, if a giant star bursts and causes a supernova, a mega explosion, we'll all be in trouble. Scientists say it won't matter if there is an early-warning system or not. It won't matter if the odds are less than being involved in the crash of a jetliner. Some astronomers believe that should this happen, we won't have to worry about loss of the ozone layer. Why? A blast of X rays will burn off the earth's atmosphere and we'll instantly be mortally singed from the supernova, or else we'll simply be fried by the sun much like an egg on a blistering sidewalk.

Another source of fear is the Swift-Tuttle comet, which was seen during the Civil War but didn't make much news when it passed 110 million miles from earth on November 7, 1972. It will be seen again in skies near us on August 14, 2126, however, and science reporters for the Washington Post News Service say that if its "jets" (burning gases on the surface of the nucleus of the comet) tilt the wrong way, the comet's course could be altered just enough to inflict the maximum penalty on us. That is, a direct hit. However, others downplay the possibility and believe that some simply enjoy indulging in cosmic alarm.

THE SCIENTIFIC END

Doomsday watchdogs do perform a valuable service to humanity, alerting us to potential disasters and exposing destructive problems. However, their use of scare tactics and fright campaigns, and terms such as the "nuclear winter" and "population bomb," tend to win converts without sufficient investigation or debate. This is the argument of some of the more conservative scientific groups.

Martin H. Krieger, associate professor of planning at the University of Southern California, explains that alarmists' reaction to problems may actually do more harm than good. "Doomsday predictions tend to substitute anxiety and fear for prudence and reason. And that substitution can itself be a prescription for disaster or at least for authoritarian government."

Those Doomsday predictions that are meant to get people moving in order to solve a problem or are used as a call to action can frighten some men and women so much that they are unable to budge. For example, if we'll someday all die in a terrible earthquake, why bother to shore up a water heater, have a battery-operated flashlight near the bed or a few days' worth of canned or dried food on hand?

Scientists, environmentalists, astronomers and earth watchers disagree on many things. Often they use as many scare tactics as possible to make the public aware of what our world faces. However, on one issue they're in unison: If humanity chooses, we can surely do away with ourselves, quite nicely, thank you very much, even without the help of Jesus Christ, the Good Lord or any other spiritual beings, including alien Space Brothers.

These are scary thoughts. They're enough to keep most of us from resting well, and as we near the millennium, Doomsday is on everybody's mind. Yet a glimmer of hope continues, and though the earth is being battered by humanity, it is still capable of recovering if we give it half a chance. There are hopeful signs, and societies have been known to radically and quickly change their attitudes when faced with a terrible alternative like the End.

In chapter 9, we'll tackle the topic of preparing for the End as it creeps ever closer. We'll find out what Main Street U.S.A. has to say about facing the finality of human existence and what Billy Graham, the Vatican and Hal Lindsey are saying too. And they've got a lot to say about our limited future on planet Earth.

*Whenever a preacher or writer begins to interpret current
events in light of Bible teachings, we need to hold up the
reality filter: It is speculation or at best assumption.*
—THE REVEREND ED HINSON,
END TIMES, THE MIDDLE EAST & THE NEW WORLD ORDER

9

ON OUR MARK, GET SET, GO?

*I*s an informed citizen of the world better prepared for the End than one who willy-nilly goes along daily with little thought to Doomsday? Maybe so. At least that's what Christians, Catholics and Jews believe. Doomsday expert Mary Stewart Relfe believes it too.

In this chapter we'll take a look at public opinion and the End and see how groups are preparing for, or attempting to prevent, their personal demise.

First, let's stop the Doomsday clock and take a minute to examine some off-the-mark prophecies of recent times. Like fashions and fads, End Time prophecies are sometimes uniquely recycled when a whole new generation begins to dread the End.

Some may even seem familiar. As we approach the year 2000, it's a good bet that we'll see some of these End Times announcements making headlines on the evening news.

THE FINAL DAYS ARE HERE AGAIN

It is impossible not to look on the doomsayers of 50, 100 or 1,000 years ago and smirk. Looking back, one can broadly smile at the End Times miscalculations. The End didn't happen—we're still here. Like Dave Barry, the humorist, wrote, "The doomsayers have goofed. But, hey, it's not the end of the world!"

Reginald Dunlop, a fundamentalist and author of numerous books on Doomsday, has predicted that famine will be so widespread as we approach the End that people will do anything. In his books, he predicts that your local butcher shop will begin to stock more than beef, chicken and pork. He sees the addition of human body parts to the butcher's inventory in order to feed the starving hordes. (Supposedly, he also knows the date when the Antichrist will appear and that of the Rapture, too.)

However, the famine that was going to starve Americans was scheduled to occur in 1986, as outlined in Dunlop's books. The Antichrist's earthly presence was to be revealed "around the year 1989 or 1990, perhaps sooner." The Rapture was to take place in 1991. Although Dunlop and his followers were ardent and eager for the End, the heavens didn't cooperate as he had foretold.

Historically and contemporarily, as we've seen, Dunlop was not alone in providing off-the-mark End Times predictions. Russell Chandler, writing in *Doomsday: The End of the World,* infers that many of the prophets should be given the "Chicken Little Award." They've kept saying, "The sky is falling; the sky is falling," but it has yet to fall.

Henry Kresyler, leader of the Watchman in the Wilderness, a Desert Hot Springs, California, Doomsday group produced dates and the schedules of events for his followers. In a multi-tape prophecy collection sold to members and interested survivalists through various Christian magazines, he includes a "last days" chart of events which are supposedly geared to the fulfillment of prophecies signaling the End. Before the tapes were updated, he called the chart a "proposed scenario for the End of this present evil age." Among items, the charts gave the date when the Soviets would invade Israel (in 1988, although it didn't happen). He marks the horrifying catastrophe of Chernobyl as a "trumpet" described in the Book of Revelation. He listed the Rapture of his church to be slated for 1991 (although that had to be revised) and Armageddon is scheduled for 1995.

Fundamentalist prophecy teacher Mary Stewart Relfe, author of the best-selling *When Your Money Fails* and *The New Money System*, asserts that the Antichrist is here, alive and doing fine among us. Not a financial expert, she claims that her writing is guided by the Holy Spirit. Relfe scribbled an A-list of potential Antichrists that includes Jimmy Carter, Henry Kissinger, King Juan Carlos of Spain and Pope John Paul II.

Relfe wrote, "After giving much time to studying the scriptural qualifications, characteristics, and prerequisite, my prudent assessment is that President Anwar Sadat of Egypt is either history's nearest prototype or the real Mr. '666.' " It became obvious that Relfe's prediction had a hole in it when Sadat was assassinated in 1981. (The "666" is a reference to the Antichrist in the Revelation. Historians tell us that it may have come from a numerology system developed by Pythagoras.)

That gentle southerner from Georgia, international peace negotiator and former president of the United States Jimmy Carter, wasn't off the hook just yet, even if Relfe left him alone. Doomsday soothsayer Doug Clark announced in 1976 on the television show "Shockwaves of Armageddon," that Carter was the ultimate evildoer predicted in the Bible, i.e., "the little horn" (Dan.

7:8, 8:9), "the man of lawlessness" (2 Thess. 2:3), and "the beast out of the sea" (Rev. 13:1, 11-18; 19:20). Clark warned that Carter would cause the "death of the United States." It would be the right time when we would see "and the Birth of one world government under President Carter." This is a reference to the European Community and Common Market, discussed in Chapter 10, and believed to be a fulfillment of biblical prophecy.

In William M. Alnor's well-done book *Soothsayers of the Second Advent*, the author identifies this technique of satanic finger-pointing as a game of "pin the tail on the antichrist." He explains that accusation is a favorite game among Doomsday prophets and that even astrologer and columnist Jeane Dixon has had her hand in it. In his book *The Genesis of Holocaust*, author Henry R. Hall quoted Dixon as saying that the Antichrist would be exactly 30 years old on February 5, 1992.

Here are some other contemporary End Times predictions that have missed the target.

* In *February 1982* the *End Times News Digest* predicted that the U.S. would be at war with the Soviets before the end of '83, and in April 1982, it claimed the great tribulation would begin "within weeks."

* After the thawing of the Cold War, overpopulation was thought to be the Doomsday culprit. Anne and Paul Ehrlich's book *The Population Bomb*, a huge best-seller, informed readers that the End could come in 1993, after uncontrollable pollution, wild overpopulation and resource depletion. By 1992 there would be no oil left on the planet.

* Edgar C. Whisenant, a former NASA engineer, told the world Christ would rapture the true church to heaven in September 1988. This earth-shattering information was published in his best-selling book

88 Reasons Why the Rapture Will Be in 1988. Whisenant boasted that he had incontrovertible proof that his date for Christ's return in 1988 was correct and that only if the Bible *was* wrong could he be wrong. (When it became obvious that he *was* wrong, Whisenant changed the date to January 1989, then later changed it to September 1989. No new date has ever been set.)

* Hal Lindsey (*The Late Great Planet Earth*) also predicted that the stop sign to humankind would be erected in 1988. He has since stated that perhaps he was too impetuous in setting a date. His new books do not forecast a specific year, but rather include a general statement that the End will be in sight about the year 2000.

* Mary Stewart Relfe was told in prayer that the End would begin in 1989. The year would include a great war that would envelop the planet. She also said that the Tribulation would begin in 1990.

* According to Relfe, Jesus Christ will come back in 1997, "just after Armageddon." She predicts that the United States will be totally destroyed within four years after that date.

THE END TIMES GAMES

What do fiber optics, the Gulf War, supermarket bar codes and your VISA card have in common? According to the contemporary prophets of End Times, these are signals that the Antichrist has already assumed power.

Mary Stewart Relfe believes, as some other fringe Christian groups do, that the supermarket bar codes help to keep track of

our money and what we're doing, buying and participating in. The
Antichrist knows what we're doing and when we're doing it, too,
thanks to the zebra code now gracing everything from toothpaste
to tomatoes.

Relfe believes the Antichrist will eventually do away with
credit cards and order a stripped code tattooed on every citizen of
the world. Most people who embrace this theory believe the tattoo
will either be on the forehead or the right hand. (This is a popular
End Times rumor that circulates among Christian groups every few
years. Look for this one to resurface soon.)

The charge card you love the most could be another tracking
device, according to Relfe and some Fundamentalists. In her
enormously successful 1982 book *The New Money System*, she
tells us that VISA is controlled by the Antichrist (MasterCard was
subject to a similar proclamation). To prove her message, she used
the following logic and wrote, "VISA is 666; Vi, the Roman
Numeral, is 6, the 'zz' sound, Zeta, the 6th character in the Greek
alphabet, is 6; a, English is 6 [implying that the letter *a* turned
backward is a 6]." She went on to find those evil sixes in everything
from bank statements to the Apollo mission, using such logic as
the following:

* Apollo has six letters.
* Each astronaut's name had six letters (Lovell, Anders
  and Borman: 666.)
* The moon trip took six days.
* The Apollo flight's gross weight came in at six
  million pounds.

Using Relfe's numerology system, almost anything could
include sixes. Yet, many Christian sects and cults jumped on her
Doomsday bandwagon and some are still jumping. Her ideas are

still quoted by evangelical preachers and Christians in order to prove that we are living in the Eve of Destruction.

A contemporary but more conservative colleague of Relfe's, Dr. James McKeever, was quoted in *The End Times News Digest* in 1981 at the height of the first 666 scare. McKeever assured his readers that the "sign of the beast" scare was groundless and illogical. He told readers that whenever he spoke to Christian groups, people pleaded to know if their VISAs and MasterCards should be destroyed. They wanted to know if their use of the plastic charge cards was somehow contributing to the end of the world.

"There is so much misinformation being put forth from well-meaning Christian broadcasters and authors," said McKeever, "that it would require several books to set the record straight. All I can hope to do [is] to try to help [people] get rid of any fear that they may have and let God replace it with His peace."

Another fascinating theory of the Antichrist involves the use of fiber optics. Did you know that this incredible invention of modern communications was at one time supposedly in use by the Antichrist? In 1979, the preachers Emil Gaverluk and Patrick Fisher of the Southwest Radio Church wrote of this in detail in *Fiber Optics: Eye of the Antichrist*. They told readers that the devil was watching the population of the world through every single television set. (Fiber optics are used in the transmission of information by light pulses along hair-thin glass fibers. Cables of optical fibers can be made smaller and lighter than conventional cables using copper wires or coaxial tubes and carry more information. Optical fibers are useful in transmitting large amounts of data between computers and for carrying data-intensive television pictures or many simultaneous telephone conversations. They are also being used in automobiles and aircraft, along with a myriad of other applications. They cannot, according to scientists and engineers, be used as demonic peep holes.)

Texe Marrs in his book *Millennium* uses persuasive and powerful Fundamental Christian rhetoric to describe the

forthcoming destruction of our world. As with many Doomsday
Christians, he adds plenty of contemporary zest to the End Times
picture, including a scenario in which the Soviet Union regains
power and wars with the Middle East.

As Otto Friedrich explained in *The End of the World*, solemn
predictions of the earth's final days have accompanied natural and
man-made catastrophes through the ages, from the sacking of
Rome to the massacres of the Holocaust. New military technology
has added to our fears; now there are even more ways for humanity
to destroy itself. Cults seem to thrive on associating each
devastating event with a prophecy. Prime examples are the killing in
the Middle East, the Gulf War and Saddam Hussein as the
Antichrist. All these events seem to be ushering in the End Times
as prophets of Doom use them to "prove" their hypotheses.

ARMED AND READY

Keep those guns loaded and the shelters ready. This is the way
that one End Times cult is preparing for the End.

The Church Universal and Triumphant (CUT) has built
fallout shelters and is stockpiling supplies and ammunition to keep
followers safe at the End. CUT believes that to sustain themselves
at the End, followers will need more than freeze-dried food. They'll
also need military weapons, elaborate survival skills and, of course,
those fallout shelters when the "big one" hits.

CUT is a branch of the "I AM" Ascended Masters, a
movement that began in the 1930s with founder Guy Ballard and
his wife Edna Ballard. The I AM movement is based on the
philosophies discussed by Madame Blavatsky and her Theosophy
movement, whom we met in Chapter 4.

Through psychic channeling, Ballard is said to have received
messages from Jesus and Saint Germain (a seventeenth-century

occultist, not the Roman Catholic Saint Germain or Germanus). His messages attracted as many as 3.5 million followers worldwide. Upon Ballard's death, Edna declared that her spouse was now a master, too—right up there with Jesus, the Apostles and Saint Germain.

Most converts accepted this pronouncement without question, just as they had accepted other dictates from the leader. However, that blind approval changed when the sect began to suspect wrongdoing. When Edna and son Donald were accused of mail fraud and fraudulent solicitation of funds, the sect's numbers dwindled, but it did not die. While the movement's importance declined, the theory of the "I Am" presence of God within continued to grow and became firmly established in the American cult experience. Various other sects have sprouted from Ballard's theories.

The Church Universal and Triumphant is the most famous of the "I AM" splinter groups. Founded in 1958 by Mark L. Prophet, whose work is now carried on by his widow, Elizabeth Clare Prophet, the group is considered one of the largest and most influential D day survivalist sects. On their 28,000-acre ranch, formerly owned by Malcolm Forbes, near Corwin Springs, Montana, the followers horde food and stockpile weapons for the End.

Severely criticized by Fundamentalist Christian groups as everything from way off base to demonic, CUT sees itself as the one true church. Individuals are asked to follow the teachings of the Ascended Masters (one of whom is now Mark L. Prophet, who speaks as a prophet called Lanello) and adhere to the sect's rituals and philosophies. Mrs. Prophet, sometimes called Ma Guru, has written many books on the philosophies of CUT, including *The Lost Years of Jesus*; many New Age counselors and ministers recommend her books for extensive study. The leaders of CUT, headed by Prophet, teach that America embodies the new promised land for the lost 10 tribes of Israel and members are the keepers of the flame. Her teachings and books are well-respected in many New Age circles.

CUT has long predicted the End and continues to prepare for Armageddon. In an essay in *U.S. News and World Report* published in 1990, William F. Allman interviewed Prophet regarding the End. She told readers that April 23, 1990, had marked the beginning of a new turn in the "Dark Cycle," a time when negative Karma "will come crashing down." Another spokesperson for the church insisted that Prophet will never, ever predict the End. They assert that they never have.

However, back in March 1989, thousands left jobs, family, friends and possessions. Like doomsayers of the past, they flocked to the compound in Montana and huddled together awaiting the news that the End had come. One night, they all rushed to the shelters. After hours hidden in the concrete quarters, the leaders informed them they could leave; it was "just a drill."

Prophet also predicted that the Soviet *glasnost* was merely a ruse to put "America the vulnerable" off guard for a surprise attack. Critics of the movement say this is only one example of the fear tactics used to support CUT's ardor for the End.

Interestingly enough, the IRS recently struck a bargain with CUT by which the organization's tax-exempt status would be returned (they are a big moneymaking association) in return for disposal of the arsenal of military-style weapons, including semiautomatic rifles, armored personnel carriers and thousands of rounds of ammunition. Additionally, CUT agreed to prohibit anyone convicted of a felony from having access to weapons on the property. Uncle Sam revealed that the church's vice president and various members pleaded guilty for using false names and addresses to procure weapons. Members may now keep guns in their homes and bring them back into the shelters "in the event of an actual nuclear war or similar emergency."

Although the surprise attack by the now-defunct Soviet Union never happened, the believers have not been dissuaded. Like other Doomsday groups, CUT is still waiting for the End, perhaps pointing a finger at another "enemy."

Prophet says that we've been safe so far because of the work provided by her and her followers. In other words, those love-our-planet-and-make-it-better thoughts are at work.

"Our important mission in Montana is to hold the balance in terms of earth changes, earthquakes, and so forth," she says, "We've done that with our mantras and our Violet Flame decrees." (Violet Flame, according to Prophet, is the cleansing principle of the Holy Spirit that protects us from the bad karma that might keep an initiate from joining the Godhead. And a mantra is a holy word, phrase or verse used in Eastern religious techniques. The mantra's vibration when spoken aloud is said to lead the meditator into unison with the divine source within.)

Currently waiting for the End on a vast parcel of land in Montana, Prophet and her followers are heartened by their ability to escape nuclear devastation, earthquakes and other disasters. On the estate there are elaborate bunkers, military weapons and enough food and supplies to outlast any End Times attempt at annihilation and to usher in the new world. Prophet now has over 30,000 followers worldwide and believes the End will take place between the early 1990s and the year 2002. That's because centuries of negative karma are supposed to come crashing down during this period.

WHAT MAIN STREET PREDICTS

America is a nation with opinions. Americans will voice their convictions without hesitation. One of the other rights we love to exercise, along with freedom of speech, is practicing our religious beliefs in the way we see fit. Or by not practicing religion at all. "There's no way any Big Brother is goin' to tell me I have to stop praying—or to pray, for that matter" is a common feeling. Freedom of religion is a cornerstone of our heritage. While some things have changed, that freedom hasn't. In our multicultural and multiethnic society, religious views are as varied as the folks inhabiting all 50 states. Their views about the End are just as divergent.

In the 1930s, when the first surveys were conducted regarding Americans' religious beliefs, 4 in 10 adults reported that they attended religious services on a regular basis. That's the same percentage as today. However, while the majority of our neighbors do not attend a church, a synagogue or a faith meeting regularly, the majority still believe in the promise of the End.

According to a 1989 survey conducted by George Gallup, Jr. and Jim Castelli:

* Nine out of ten Americans say they have never doubted the existence of God.
* Eight out of ten Americans believe God still works miracles.
* Seven out of ten believe in a life after death.
* With the intense curiosity indicated from the plethora of books and television shows about angels, it's obvious that Americans believe in them, too.
* Eight Americans in ten say they believe in a final judgment and a time when they'll be required to answer for their sins.

Whether this Judgment comes after death or when the End arrives, most Americans hold the belief that they must somehow be prepared. They have to get ready either for their personal end or the end of our planet. Significant differences exist between various religious faiths, however. For instance, while 87 percent of

Protestants and 85 percent of Catholics believe in Judgment Day, only 37 percent of Jews surveyed share those views.

Among Protestants, 96 percent of Evangelicals and 80 percent of non-Evangelicals say they believe in Judgment Day. Black and white Evangelicals equally share that view, with 96 percent of each believing in the accountability of sins. Among non-Evangelical Protestants, however, 90 percent of blacks and 79 percent of whites believe in Judgment Day.

Whether one believes in Judgment Day and the End, the number of supporters decreases as the educational level rises. The surveyors found out that 91 percent of those who hadn't graduated from high school believed. Eighty-six percent of high school graduates, 74 percent of those with some college and 66 percent of college graduates believed and accepted the idea that they'd personally face God on Judgment Day.

In the future, there will probably be more diversity in religion and the institutional church will not be as firm. George Gallup believes that "Americans will continue to be unique, with an unmatched combination of high levels of education and high levels of religious belief and activity."

Apparently, they'll keep believing in the End, too.

WHAT CHRISTIANS HOPE

Many Christians and their church leaders do not believe in the literal Second Coming as written in the Book of Revelation. They do honor the words and the poetry and the drama and use it for lessons of their faith. However, they don't believe that Jesus Christ will physically appear on the earth.

Generally, more liberal, mainstream ministers teach their flocks that Christ has returned or will return to us mortals spiritually. Some believe this is accomplished when one accepts

Him into one's life; this is the fulfillment of the prediction of his return as foretold in Revelation. Therefore, those mainstreamers are *not* into predicting D day as the end of all of us.

Another group teaches that, yes, Jesus may return, but they do not spend much energy or enthusiasm on the details of that return. They're just getting ready spiritually while working in this world.

Those who predict the End as sketched in the Bible point out that the apostle Peter warned that in the last days (just before Christ's real return) false teachers try to convince their followers that if He were going to return, it would have already happened. They quote: "Where is the promise of His coming? For ever since the fathers [apostles] fell asleep, all continues just as it was from the beginning of creation" (2 Peter 3:4).

This is the message of many American Christians who are preparing for the return. Concerning the argument that the only coming will be within each personal spirit, they stress that one out of every 25 verses in the New Testament is related to the Second Coming of Christ and the events leading up to it. They look to the literal translation of the Bible for confirmation that survival of humanity and the fulfillment of the promises made to the believing remnant of the Jewish race are dependent on Christ's return.

Hal Lindsey, a Fundamentalist whose views have been integrated into mainstream religious beliefs, writes, "As a matter of fact, in the Old Testament there were more than three hundred prophecies regarding Christ's first coming, all of which were literally fulfilled." Lindsey and other Christians who believe in the End point out that there are in excess of five hundred biblical comments and prophecies related to Christ's second visit.

Jerry Falwell, one of the country's most visible ministers, chancellor of Liberty University and an outspoken supporter of the Moral Majority, believes that America is about to have a true spiritual awakening. He supports the theory that God will grant us a last reprieve. When God does postpone the End, according to

Falwell, it will be for one purpose: to accept the gospel of Jesus Christ. Like other Fundamentalists, he's waiting and praying for the End. Falwell has been publicizing, preaching and spreading End Times prophecies since well before his days of attending National Security Council briefings at the request of President Reagan. Nuclear war, he insists, is inevitable. The end is inescapable, Falwell says, "But we [believers] will not be here for Armageddon."

The Reverend Billy Graham, practically an American institution, believes that we are living in the final days. He sees events leading straight toward the exit door, with no detour in sight. In 1983, Graham wrote in *Approaching Hoofbeats: The Four Horsemen of the Apocalypse*, that it was quite possible we would shortly experience "nuclear conflagrations, biological holocausts and chemical apocalypses rolling over the earth, bringing man to the edge of the precipice." Unlike other Doomsayers, Graham has been careful to avoid date setting. During the Persian Gulf War, in 1991, he told *Los Angeles Times* columnist Russell Chandler that there was something more sinister happening than just a war, alluding to the destiny of humanity as planned in the Bible and of the appearance of the Antichrist. He said the upheaval in the Middle East could have "major spiritual implications. These events are happening in that part of the world where history began, and, the Bible says, where history as we know it will someday end." Graham added that he wouldn't want to actually predict that we are nearing the end of time, the end of this age, although he revealed, "I personally think we are."

It is generally thought by those Americans who teach the End Times gospel that there will be a terrible and cataclysmic tribulation followed by the War of Armageddon. However, most Christians believe they will not have to face the horrifying situation. They believe it will take place before the Antichrist rises up to rule and Jesus will appear from the heavens to rapture (transport) his believers out of our world. They are praying for deliverance.

While Christians discuss, wait and pray, other religious leaders return to the Bible to interject their dogmas. It is interesting to learn as we hear the interpretations of the Scriptures that Jesus never taught the principles of escapism from the world or from worries. Jesus's Great Commission (Matt. 28:18-19) is to go to all nations and bring the message of the Gospel. Jesus walked among the common people including the "undesirables" and the unclean. Rather than discuss how the good will be raptured when times get tough, Jesus taught and prayed for his disciples so that they would be protected from the evil while in the world (John 17:15).

The apostle Paul took on a missionary effort that became a worldwide movement. Modern Christian theologians, including the respected Reverends George Mather and Larry A. Nichols, explain that the real mission of the church, of Paul and of Christians is to make a difference in the world in which we physically reside. Like many, they believe that humanity must work for change among those who need the message. The authors say, "Indeed, the Christian should take more seriously than anyone else the importance of taking care of the environment, seeking peace, playing an active role in government, etc., because the Christian knows that this world was created by God."

SAVING ONE'S SPACE

It is absorbing to consider the attraction to Doomsday and the possibilities for the millennium. Whether the words come from a Bible-slapping preacher on the Trinity Network or a recluse walking down New York's Fifth Avenue, the future is out of our hands. Like other cults and societies of the past, should we simply do what they did and give up? What of the philosophy of "It's gonna end anyhow, so why fight it?"

If this is true, then maybe we can go back to dumping chemicals in the Mississippi, allowing factories to belch smoke and filth into the air, and watch as the innocents of the world are slaughtered by despotic warlords. The bottom line with this Doomsday train of thought is, of course, that it might be easier to give up. If one takes the alternate view, then there's work to be done. Humanity must get busy with the work required in an attempt to rectify our ecological mistakes, stop the global contamination, check the killing madness and strive to mend the world that we've inherited.

The visions of the End are endlessly intriguing. Often it seems like we have little choice in the matter, but the flicker of optimism can be kindled. Many ecologically oriented and spiritual groups have a plan. The strategy is to take charge of one's health, happiness and environment. Saving one's own space may be the only way to survive in the fragile years ahead.

It's easy to shirk off responsibility. That's somebody else's trash in the street, we tell ourselves, or another country's rusting nuclear warhead, another state's polluted river or another person's starving brother, sister or child. It's easy to find excuses not to get involved. And it's easy to blame the government, global warming or the Antichrist. The hard part of moving into the year 2000 and beyond may be taking personal responsibility for one's actions and life and for one's own planet.

World watchers, caring citizens of the planet and possibly your neighbors are already actively involved in the do-it-ourselves project to save the earth. Will it work? Who's to say? The result of even a small effort will be revealed only when the final hand of history is dealt.

Lao-tzu, the legendary Chinese philosopher, said, "The journey of 1,000 miles begins with a single step." With the philosophy of making the most of every day but planning for the future, one person can do a lot.

As we dream of the future, many are lost to a hopelessness that nearly paralyzes our desires and their goals. How can we visualize a bright future when the present seems so bleak?

This is the topic for the next chapter. We'll examine what happens when there is little hope of a rosy tomorrow and when prophecies fail. We'll take another optimistic stance and see what the world's futurists are planning as we move ever closer to the closing of this millennium.

> *Unless we can find some way*
> *to keep our sights on tomorrow,*
> *we cannot expect to be in touch with today.*
> —DEAN RUSK, FORMER U. S. SECRETARY OF STATE

10

DOOMSDAY JEOPARDY: THE FUTURE OF THE FUTURE

Humankind has somehow learned to survive on the brink of eradication. Those who moan that it can't get worse will give an example, a moment later, of how it could.

We've talked about the disgruntled Millerites who splintered off into other sects, and the rise of New Age spiritualism. We've heard from scientists and skeptics and pole shifters and sleeping prophets. And we've examined the cults that seem to spontaneously spring to life then (sometimes) disappear.

As we approach the year 2000, we are bound to see more Doomsday groups coming into the limelight. What will happen to them if the millennium doesn't usher in the End? We can get a good idea by examining what happens when the history of prophecies failed, and we'll do so later in the chapter. We'll also ponder how we are to consider the future if, in fact, we have no future. Finally, we'll turn a deaf ear to the Doomsayers and see what the futurists believe will happen if we make it past the fateful 2000. And because most of us love or wish for happy endings, we'll attempt to finish our examination of Doomsday on a joyful note. As the old saying goes, It's always darkest before the dawn. Lately, as you already know, it's been pretty dark.

THE END OF HISTORY

The history of the world's End Times theories is too vast for one book to do it justice. Throughout these pages, the choice of what to select and share with readers, what to skim over and what to ignore has been an immense weight. Certain people, places and events can almost be heard screaming for more detailed descriptions. Yet there hasn't been room.

Most of the Doomsday theories, whether they are ecological, New Age or biblical, are pretty darn scary. Often the theories leave little on which to hang a few hopes. It isn't even that comforting to remind ourselves that past End Times movements have failed. Sure, the End didn't come, but those who prayed and waited for the End quite often received what they wished for. It was *their* end. The same could happen with regard to clean water, clean air and sufficient food for the world community. Doomsaying prophets and followers believe anyone who looks past the year 2000 with any hope is deluding himself or herself. A book on Doomsday doesn't leave much room for humanity to cheer.

But wait!

Among the avalanche of doom and gloom that's heading our way, there is a tiny flicker of light. It seems as though it might ignite into a bona fide bonfire of hope regarding the years ahead. Looking at ourselves, even under a microscope, we must admit that people are optimistic. Just recently, we've seen that characteristic in the survivors of weather-torn Florida, devastated war zones and refugee camps in Africa, the Baltic countries and the Caribbean.

If there was no spark of faith in the future, who among us would choose to bear children, go to work, save for a rainy day or retirement or plan vacations? Who would have the courage to dig themselves out of an earthquake-crumbled building, trek over fields littered with explosives or surmount any of the other incredible obstacles people overcome to stay alive? People are optimistic. People are survivors. There are plenty of people out there who are cheerful and confident about the turn of the century and the future of planet Earth.

Yet some theologians and sociologists say that as we approach the year 2000 a strange paralysis seems to have seized our thinking. Rather than moving ahead and creating solutions to our problems, we are gripped by a malaise that began several decades ago. (Some people believe this is why funding for the space program has diminished.) Many believe that we are actually dreading and/or are unable to think about the future. A kind of fatalism has settled on the West, and America in particular.

Do we believe in a future existence? Do we believe in one that may not be a duplicate of the American dream? According to the principles of the Bible, without having faith in the future, we will perish. Theologians point out that not having notions of life in the future can quickly immerse a society in self-indulgence. Some people attribute the inability to believe in the future to a severe lack of vision.

WHEN A PROPHECY FAILS

Will the End turn out to be like a party at which the guest of honor never shows? What will happen to the mass consciousness of the planet if the End doesn't arrive? According to social scientists, when a prophecy is born, flourishes and eventually fails, the leader and the group go through specific stages. By knowing the steps, perhaps we can better cope with disappointment if Doomsday doesn't arrive. Maybe "Doomsday stress management" will be the hip new handle we'll cling to as we reach the end of the century.

It's a curious fact of life that when a person believes in a cause or a philosophy with his or her complete body and soul, even facts won't budge the believer. A person with a conviction is a tough person to change. This is the paradox of followers who believe in End Times. End Times failure often follows a certain sequence of events. While the standard sequences do not always match nor are all the steps always taken, according to theologians and sociologists typically, they usually follow this scheme.

* Initially, there is a revelation or the expounding of a deep conviction by a leader. This may be a personal discovery after a dream or channeled information from a spiritual or God source, such as with Edgar Cayce, Nostradamus, the Fatima prophecy (and other Marian visions) and John in the Book of Revelation. Or it may be based on study, such as the teachings of Montanus, William Miller, Charles Taze Russell and Hal Lindsey.

* The conviction must have current relevance. Whether one believes in ecological or Christian Doomsday, for example, the conviction helps the person explain present circumstances and the consequences of present actions.

❋ The prophet, leader or messiah must show that he or she is committed to the cause. A millionaire could give away his or her wealth and become an itinerant minister, or a glamorous actor retreat from society and take up residence in a cave. The leader may stop shaving, dress in rags (to indicate humility and honor Jesus, a supreme being or the ancient cosmic ancestors), refuse to eat meat and spend 24 hours a day praying. In this way he or she is set apart from the masses. It doesn't hurt to sermonize and proclaim the End in loud, clear terms at every possible opportunity and that he or she is the long-awaited messiah.

❋ The belief must be specific to gather a group into the fold. As with the year 1000, the year 2000 is very specific to people of our generation. Or there may be a date-setting attempt, such as the multitude of dates set by the leaders of Jehovah's Witnesses. At other times, an eclipse, a drastic seasonal change, a flood or a strange occurrence may provide a specific event on which to tie a prophecy of the End. When Muntzer of Munster, Germany (discussed in chapter 3), spoke to a crowd of eight thousand destitute peasants during the End Times revolt of 1525, which he masterminded, a rainbow appeared. It dazzled the crowd and may have dazzled Muntzer, too. The rainbow had become Muntzer's symbol and this rallied the starving, unhappy and illiterate peasants into action. They believed the rainbow was a sign from God that Muntzer had His blessing. (Shortly thereafter, the German princes ordered their troops to fire on the crowd, slaughtering thousands. The horse soldiers stampeded the poor, killing some, dispersing the others. Muntzer narrowly escaped the killing fields, but only for a short time. It wasn't long before he was tracked down, tortured and beheaded.)

✳ These first five conditions can bring a group together and cement them to the cause behind a charismatic leader. Often, as with the Millerites, the movement becomes self-perpetuating. It may seem to take on a life of its own with fractions springing up spontaneously. As the group gathers steam, the prophet becomes more powerful. He or she will often appoint apostles to help spread the word of the event, such as the end of the world comes next Tuesday at 3 P.M. As with some millennial sects, like the Mormons, missionaries are sent throughout the world to convert believers and get them ready for the end. The Millerites spread across the country holding massive revival meetings, baptisms and converting as many as possible before the Final day.

✳ Sometimes there is "secret" knowledge available to believers. It may be the exact date of the End. The uninitiated must be initiated before the knowledge is shared. This can be through a Christian baptism, for instance, or a cosmic induction for a group believing in UFO abduction and waiting for the Space Brothers to make themselves evident. Often this information is closely guarded, making it seem all the more important.

✳ After a period of missionary work and conversion takes place, the group focuses directly on the End. There may be intense studying of the scriptures, specific ceremonies or rituals, or dressing in a special manner, as with the Millerite ascension robes. Sometimes believers stop planting crops or kill off their meat supply.

* Generally, it is at this point that the group comes together to wait, as the Church of Universal Triumph did when it retreated to the fallout shelters in Montana. Preaching to the outside world may halt as believers focus on the final days and hours. Some groups withdraw to undesirable, inaccessible places. A shocking, contemporary example is the religious End Times disaster involving the 930 followers of the Peoples Temple prophet Jim Jones. They tramped through inhospitable jungle to establish a Guyanese retreat as they waited for the end. During the period of 1972 through 1978, they believed that Jones was the messiah. Period. End of discussion. In the dedication of surrendering their wills and minds, they drank poisoned punch on November 18, 1978, in a mass suicide. As Russell Chandler pointed out in the *Los Angeles Times*, "Nearly all who perished were convinced that the death they were about to experience would be glorious compared to the apocalyptic hell that their megalomanic leader had assured would overtake them if they remained alive."

  When groups totally withdraw from society, they often come under the suspicion of established church groups and governments. Sometimes the suspicions are justified, as with the Branch Davidians and CUT, who had to relinquish their military-style weaponry that was being stockpiled for defense tasks when the tribulation took a turn for the worse.

* Then the specific event passes. When the End does not come, the prophecy is disconfirmed.

* What happens next varies from one group to the next. Some groups fall apart. Others gain momentum with

the initial disconfirmation. Public ridicule or disgrace
may ignite an even stronger commitment. The zealous
actions of fellow believers make it even more difficult
to withdraw from the movement. Many followers are
too shamed to admit that they doubt the leader or
have done useless things for the good of the cause,
such as selling their house and giving the money to
the movement.

The Jehovah's Witnesses, as an illustration, have
had a number of disconfirmations, yet their numbers
are stronger than ever. Likewise Jack Van Impe, first
discussed in chapter 6, with his televised and
videotaped End Times messages, has seen personal
disconfirmation but continues to gather followers.

* Finally, when it is impossible to deny that the End
hasn't occurred and won't occur, the prophet may
quietly slip out of sight or be publicly humiliated (as
with William Miller). Then the group shatters.

* But sometimes that's not the end of a Doomsday
prophecy or of a group. Often, groups spring to life
from the remains of a failed prophetic group. This
was seen in the beginnings of the Seventh-Day
Adventists and the Jehovah's Witnesses as by-
products of the Millerite movement, as well as the
resurgence of the Montanite movement seen again in
Munster, Germany, in the early 1500s.

Perhaps by taking note of such steps, we can make some
sense of current events. If we haven't self-destructed or been
raptured, come the year 2040 or beyond, some of us may look
back and chuckle at the zeal in which humanity met 2000 and
went on.

A FRESH LOOK AT THE MILLENNIUM

Many believe the year 2000 will be a time to heave a collective sigh. We will finally be able to chase away those archetypal thoughts of destruction and absolute doom. We will begin to believe that humanity may survive in spite of itself.

Experts on the future such as John Naisbitt and Patricia Aburdene, authors of the best-selling books *Megatrends* and *Megatrends 2000*, explain that the word 'millennium' is emerging as a metaphor for renewed appreciation and hope for humanity.

They write that when focusing on the millennium, it's technology we think of. There's space travel, robots, medical breakthroughs and biotechnology. And there's hope. They write, "The most exciting breakthroughs of the 21st century will occur not because of technology but because of an expanding concept of what it means to be human."

Like others who are looking forward to casting off the dismal psychological yoke of this century and are ready to dash at a breakneck speed into the next, Naisbitt and Aburdene believe that someday, in the not-too-distant future, we'll look back at this century with various intensities of horror. "Today we are emerging from a 20th-century version of the Dark Ages," they remark. This era will be thought of as a time of totalitarianism, intrusion of technology into people's privacy and of runaway industrialization. It will be a time of personal horrors and private fears. The flicker of hope referred to above, according to the authors, comes because humanity is about to enter a renaissance. There will be renewed vigor. It will be the individual who will become important, rather than the corporation, church or country, as we head into the third millennium.

Perhaps our future will prove to be a form of heaven on earth, reflecting the concepts of nirvana, heaven, utopia or bliss. This would, of course, be a validation of what some New Age doomsayers are saying. Many New Agers believe that the next century will be aglow with love, since there will be a change in the cosmic collective consciousness, an alteration of the materialism of all humankind.

Some trend watchers are certain that the millennium will produce a booming global economy that began in the 1990s, with increased free-market trading. Before long, as spirituality soars to new heights, there will be an age of religious revival, born from the dark days before the year 2000. Other forecasters predict that the millennium will be the age of feminism. We will see the privatization of the welfare state and astonishing breaks in technology. Individual thinking and the precious resource of humanity will be honored.

Many see the year 2000 and beyond as a time of awakening, of prosperity, of success in the social and ecological movements begun in the 1990s. Pollution of the major rivers of the United States, for example, has been slowed or stopped. Yes, we're still cleaning up. That will continue for quite some time. But just look at Pittsburgh. It's no longer a sooty, grimy joke of an urban mess. Rather, it's a thriving international city filled with zest for life and a rekindling of the American spirit of ingenuity.

Here are some everyday developments we can hope to see come the year 2000 and beyond:

The future in the home: With more family activities, futurist designers say family spaces, such as the kitchen, will be much more open. There will be dining areas where people can gather and eat and gather and cook. With more women involved in careers, time will be limited and a streamlined, easy-to-maintain home with easy-to-clean furnishings will be expected.

There will be an increase in the expense of buying or renting homes and apartments come the next decade; more people will be sharing digs. With the possibility of unemployment remaining at the highs currently experienced, extended families will reside under one roof and adult children will stay home longer, finishing college and establishing careers before they set out on their own.

On health: In 2000 and beyond, health care will continue to move toward preventing rather than treating sickness. Instead of deprivation diets for the obese or others who are unable to lose weight or want to have trimmer bodies, there will be medication (already in the final testing stages) to change the body's metabolism. Plastic surgery won't be reserved for the rich but will be available to anyone who wants to look and feel glamorous. However, with new creams and tonics, plastic surgery will slowly become obsolete.

Low-fat diets will be the norm as baby boomers and their adult offspring strive to maintain a healthy lifestyle. Health specialists expect to see cigarette smoking drop to an all-time low; others predict that it will be so restricted that smokers will only be able to light up in their own homes.

In the field of genetics, there will be immense advances. For instance, if a person has a genetic predisposition to a specific cancer, he or she will be able to follow a precise preventive plan to avoid the disease. Many people believe that science will find a treatment and a cure for our more terrible diseases, including cancer, AIDS and Alzheimer's.

Population experts believe that in the year 2000 and beyond, many women will postpone motherhood even further without fear of their biological clock slowing or shutting down. At a young age, probably in the late teens or early twenties, futurists believe that women will have their eggs frozen and stored in depositories. When the women are ready to conceive, the eggs will be defrosted and implanted in the mother. If the woman is too old to physically bear the child or chooses not to for career or health reasons, the egg can be implanted in a surrogate mother who will then carry the child to term. Men will deposit sperm in the same way and, like women, will be able to select the birth parent through computerized genetic selection, much like shopping for a car or a home.

In our next millennium, there will be hope for infertile couples, too, as medical discoveries enable us to treat fertility problems. Every couple who wishes to conceive will be able to do so. With the regular use of estrogen replacement therapy during and after menopause, women in the best years of their lives will become a stronger force in the community and in the workplace.

Health experts say we will no longer refer to the "aging process," because one can choose to stop maturing completely. Organ transplantation will be a normal part of this maintenance process. People will pay to have cell samples made of all their vital organs so that when one's heart, for example, needs to be replaced, it can be cloned and transplanted. Because one's own cells will be used to generate the organ, there will be no fear of rejection or death from the procedure.

Beyond 2000, prognosticators of health tell us that the human life span will be extended. There will be an end to disease. Healthy food and clean water will be plentiful. Someday in the future, you might hear, "My goodness! You don't look a day over 100!"

Another significant change that futurists envision is the aging of America's population. Many of the elderly are single. Does this mean that dating and mating in one's golden years will give rise to new social customs? Possibly so.

On spirituality: While some doomsaying groups will fade away, many trend watchers see the next century as one of true spirituality. They believe there will be a real renaissance of religion focusing on the mortal and spiritual needs of the individual. Once the End fails to occur, energy will no longer be centered on that event. In the year 2000 and beyond, humanity will reaffirm the quest of achieving a balanced life. Once more we will attempt to live by the Golden Rule. Most Americans believe that religion will play a greater role in our country after the year 2000 and that the Second Coming will happen sometime in the next thousand years.

The metaphysical community: New Age groups have been whispering about the breakdown of organized religion after the turn of the century, specifically with the dissolving of the Roman Catholic church.

In the working world: With more women in the work force, issues of child care will become non-issues, in the same way that worker-safety standards that were once "impossible" to adhere to became the rule.

There will be green zones in industrial areas where workers can walk and relax between shifts, more vacation time and health care for all workers, as even small businesses provide coverage to employees.

Two-income families will be the norm, and there will be greater sharing of family responsibilities between men and women. These "families" will not necessarily be related by marriage or blood but simply people who care about one another.

People will carry electronic communicators that include a computer, an interactive TV and a videophone, much like a Dick Tracy watch. Such devices will enable employers to keep track of their employees more easily. If a salesperson is loafing in the Hawaiian sun rather than attending a sales conference, he or she will have a hard time disguising the sights and sounds of crashing waves and people frolicking on the sand.

Many space experts believe that by the year 2020, we will see huge construction projects in outer space—that is, if taxpayers are able to support the cost. They believe that if the funding for the space shuttle program is diverted to various pioneering explorations, we could even have communities on Mars before 2025.

Forget a retirement home in Florida and a golf cart. Experts say we shouldn't expect to retire in the future. Workers will choose to embark on a new career rather than settle in a Sunbelt state. With improved nutrition and medical research, the seniors of the future will be in much better shape than ever before. Therefore, they won't want to sit back and watch TV or play bridge. Those who do "retire" will choose to volunteer, joining programs such as the Peace Corps, and remain active in the latter portion of their lives.

Because there will be a drop in the birth rate and fewer young people in the work pool, elders will be seen as an untapped American resource. Older workers will be encouraged to stay on the job. By 1999, there will be close to 100,000 people in the United States older than 100. The fastest-growing age group will be people 85 and older. And by 2025, the number of elders will double. (Marketing and advertising companies are already targeting this segment of the population.)

The lackluster and repetitious jobs of the past few decades will be turned over to robots in the future, say the future experts. The mechanized revolution that started in the eighties will only become stronger in the next century and affect every manufacturing process. The good news is that those who are ousted by machines will be retrained for the information and services industries.

The future holds great promise for the resurgence of the individual. This will be especially evident in the workplace. Entrepreneurship will be at an all-time high; networking will be everything. As technology increases, people will want to return to personally dealing with clients, and consumers will want special services provided in face-to-face relationships with shop and business owners.

Instead of minute electronic wonders keeping Big Brother's eye on everyone, as was once feared, businesspeople will be empowered by technology. While we once left the home to go to work, in the year 2000 and beyond more and more people will do business from their homes, linked by high-tech equipment that will make a fax machine look like a washboard.

Naisbitt and Aburdene are among those who believe the next century will be productive for women. They write:

> In the first decades of the third millennium we and our children will look back at the later half of the 20th century and remark on how quaint were the days when women were excluded form the top echelons of business and political leadership, much as we today recall when women could not vote. How naive were the men and women of the 1980's, we will say, those people who believed in something called a 'glass ceiling' and thought it would forever exclude women from the top.

In the community of the world: Green will be in. With more attention to the environment, experts tell us that every community will have a common area for relaxation, play and meditation. While more people may be living in high-rise apartments, everyone will take time off seriously. As more people become health-oriented, there will be softball fields and biking paths and hiking trails. Those dismal areas that were once abandoned railway lines will continue to be turned into trails for nature lovers. The demand for more national parks and nature reserves will continue as more people prefer to spend leisure time outdoors. Community parks will see changes. The benches will be made from recycled plastic materials that once held milk. The equipment on which the kids play will have once been cars and aluminum cans.

There's good news and bad news regarding the IRS and taxes. Come the year 2000, we'll still be paying income tax, experts say, with Uncle Sam most likely taking more of our hard-earned dollars. If it's any comfort, by the year 2000, we'll all be able to file electronically right from our own PCs and modems using simpler programs to figure what we should and shouldn't deduct. Audits will be unnecessary because there will be very little room for creative tax preparation.

The universal debit card, seen by some Christians as a verification of the workings of the Antichrist, will be in even greater use come the next decade. Rather than cash, we'll use it regularly for groceries, gas and gadding about. Eventually, we'll reach a point where using cash will seem old-fashioned. Consumers will think of it as too bulky for wallets and perchance as germ-ridden bits of paper.

On vacation: Travel is thought to be the growth industry of the future. But before we go somewhere, we'll be able to sample the trip through the technology of holograms, virtual reality and robotics to see if we'll enjoy the destination. When the time comes for the actual trip, flight times will be greatly reduced, since airplanes will be further from the gravitational pull of the earth during the flight and can go faster. When we arrive, we'll be able to instantly communicate in the language of the country or planet through a tiny ear communicator everyone will wear. Straight out of *Star Trek*, it will translate the language so that barriers of communication will be a nightmare of the past.

But where will we go? To the moon, Alice, some believe. NASA predicts that one day in the future, a trip to Mars will be on the agenda. For business or pleasure, we'll move into the galaxy. We may even be able to check into orbiting resorts or spas or pack up the kids for a week at Venus Disney.

Once the basic needs of life, such as shelter and safety are met in the future, we can address higher needs, such as the need to belong and to realize the self.

There will be the "prospect of general peace in the 21st century, heralded by the lifting of the nuclear arms threat in the 1990s," wrote *Time* correspondent Bruce W. Nelan in 1992. Nelan predicted that in the century ahead there will be more democracies than ever and they will dominate in Europe, the Americas and the countries of the Pacific Rim. Since democratic states typically do not make war on one another, "Warfare should become essentially irrelevant for these nations, most of which will reduce their armed forces to the minimum necessary for individual or collective defense."

MEGAMISTAKES

Predictions of the future are often filled with mistakes. Steven Schnaars, author of *Megamistakes*, a critique of technological prognostication, says that in many cases the speed of change has been exaggerated. "If you look at the forecasts for the last 10 to 20 years, the most accurate ones assume a certain constancy to the world." In the 1890s, it was predicted that by 1920, all the trees in North America would be used as fuel. Then came the use of natural gas, and the prediction was forgotten. What we are predicting now could be made totally erroneous by the advent of a new technology.

Forecasting the future is tricky business, in social as well as religious circles. Social commentators give the example of the two-way picture telephone. The technology has been available since 1969, yet it has never been accepted. (Perhaps it didn't go over since we'd have to get out of the shorts, T-shirt and sun hat before putting on a rasping voice and calling in sick on the next beautiful excuse for a sick day.) Two-way-video office meetings, well-planned and with everyone suitably attired, are just catching on.

Future analyst Faith Popcorn said that in the 1990s we'd all become couch potatoes with the arrival of the home office for workers. Yes, more people have offices in their homes, but we're still commuting. Actually, few prognosticators of the future in years past foresaw the impact that women have had in the work force or the political and social power the women's movement would have on the world.

Only one forecast for the future is a cinch: People will continue to predict what life will be like and what we'll do in the future.

WHAT CAN BE LEARNED
FROM DOOMSDAY?

The first millennium probably didn't inspire much interest in the long-term future of humanity. People were more concerned with just making it through the next day. It took everything peasants had to keep body and soul together. Few were educated enough even to consider that the End might be at hand. And if they did give it any thought, heaven might have looked pretty promising, because life in 999 A.D. was a grim struggle for survival.

What will happen as we move toward the year 2000? What can we expect? Unless something drastic changes, the media will continue to shake us up about it in order to grab viewers and ratings. And the ever-increasing plethora of End Times Christian books will continue to warn of terrible circumstances—although many will have to change their dates as we progress to 2000 and beyond.

As we approach the millennium, we may be able to scare ourselves silly about Doomsday and even bring it on ourselves. As our grandmothers' said, Be careful what you wish for; you just might get it.

Sociologists believe that a society that takes Doomsday predictions too seriously is in danger of responding in extreme and inappropriate ways. The Nazis attempted to use the predictions of Nostradamus to undermine the French resistance.

Humanity is tenacious and has learned to bounce back. This characteristic shows no sign of fading, even in the face of Doomsday. We've endured the wars and mass killings, plagues that have exterminated three quarters of the world's population and innumerable natural disasters. For instance, after the San Francisco earthquake, people hollered "Play ball!" and returned to our national pastime as soon as possible. Humanity continues to cope and to exist.

With any luck, killers like cancer and AIDS will shortly be treated as a chronic disease and not death sentences. Global warming is beginning to be understood and that's a start in rectifying the situation. And nuclear arms control continues to move toward possible monitoring in all the world.

Anne and Paul Ehrlich write that while there are no easy ways out, there are no insurmountable problems facing humanity. "There are, in short, no insuperable barriers to creating a peaceful Earth in which homo sapiens leads a rich existence without over stressing the natural systems that support human life—an Earth on which both biological and cultural evolution can proceed into the indefinite future. Unless, of course, the behavior of our species itself turns out to be such a barrier."

Our best hope lies in the fact that we can identify how our present predicament has evolved and what changes need to be made to resolve it. Perhaps there will be no miracles, no outside spiritual or supernatural intervention and no new inventions. Perhaps none is required. As earthlings, we already have the power to preserve the planet and care for it in a way that everyone wants. We simply have to be willing to exercise it and to make the plans work. A universal prayer for the year 2000 and beyond may well include a cleaner planet and a peaceful heaven on earth.

AN END TO THE END

Could what seems to be the End turn out to be a beginning? Maybe the theme of the third millennium will be "The Good Earth: Part III" and January 1, 2000 will open a new chapter in the chronology of humanity. Maybe it will be the millennium in which we prove our true resilience.

As we creep closer and closer to that mystical year 2000, we must remember that the future is a destination so close that it is arriving every second. It is so illusive that we plan for it even without planning. The future is always with us.

Destruction or utopia? It might be up to us or to a throw of the cosmic dice. Only tomorrow knows for sure.

Countdown to the End

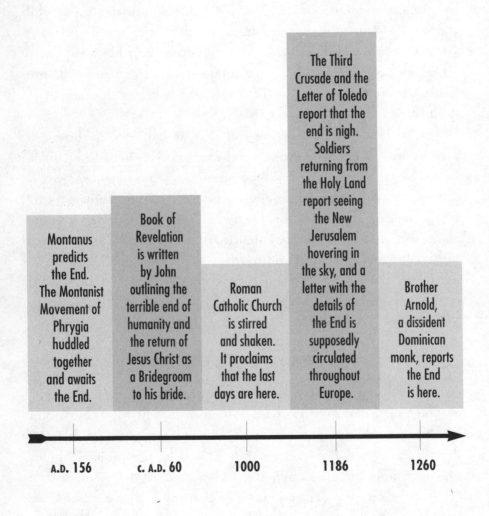

Montanus predicts the End. The Montanist Movement of Phrygia huddled together and awaits the End.

Book of Revelation is written by John outlining the terrible end of humanity and the return of Jesus Christ as a Bridegroom to his bride.

Roman Catholic Church is stirred and shaken. It proclaims that the last days are here.

The Third Crusade and the Letter of Toledo report that the end is nigh. Soldiers returning from the Holy Land report seeing the New Jerusalem hovering in the sky, and a letter with the details of the End is supposedly circulated throughout Europe.

Brother Arnold, a dissident Dominican monk, reports the End is here.

A.D. 156   c. A.D. 60   1000   1186   1260

Countdown to the End

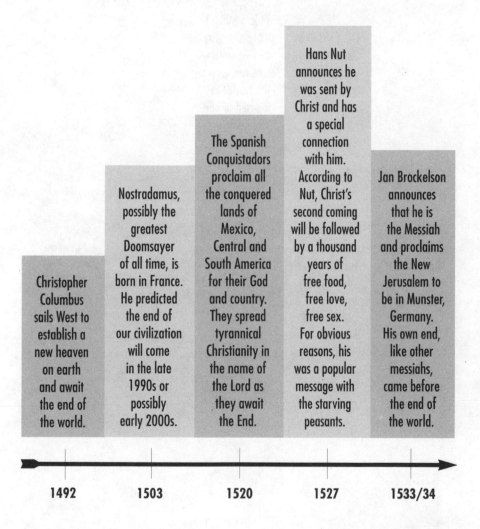

Hans Nut announces he was sent by Christ and has a special connection with him. According to Nut, Christ's second coming will be followed by a thousand years of free food, free love, free sex. For obvious reasons, his was a popular message with the starving peasants.

The Spanish Conquistadors proclaim all the conquered lands of Mexico, Central and South America for their God and country. They spread tyrannical Christianity in the name of the Lord as they await the End.

Nostradamus, possibly the greatest Doomsayer of all time, is born in France. He predicted the end of our civilization will come in the late 1990s or possibly early 2000s.

Jan Brockelson announces that he is the Messiah and proclaims the New Jerusalem to be in Munster, Germany. His own end, like other messiahs, came before the end of the world.

Christopher Columbus sails West to establish a new heaven on earth and await the end of the world.

1492   1503   1520   1527   1533/34

Countdown to the End

Pilgrims, Puritans and other settlers seek religious freedom as they establish a new world in a new land and await Jesus's return.

Early American doomsayers predict the End with all the fire and brimstone as foretold in the Bible. Shaker Mother Lee (who believed she was the Messiah) and Isaac Bullard (who supposedly dressed only in a buckskin girdle and never washed) gathered followers and spread their word regarding the End.

Prophet William Miller's final doomsday miscalculation came and went. The world was supposed to end, according to Miller and his followers, between March 21, 1843 and March 21, 1844. Millerism splinters off and forms other doomsaying religious movements, including the Jehovah's Witnesses and Seventh Day Adventists.

Christian Fundamentalists expect to be raptured at any moment, but definitely before the mystical year 2000.

Occultist Aleister Crowley informs the world that he is the feared Antichrist. Crowley believes he will reign over the terrible years of tribulation.

| 1720 | 1776 | 1844 | c. 1900 | 1904 |

Countdown to the End

Jehovah's Witnesses predict that the battle of Armageddon will happen and the world as we know it will end.	Three Italian children meet the Virgin Mother in a corn field and reveal the Fatima Prophecy. Some reports say it tells of the world's end by the year 2000 in a fiery hell reminiscent of the Book of Revelation.	Edgar Cayce announces it's countdown time. He foretells how World War II will signal our final curtain call, and by the year 2000, it will be all over.	Herbert Armstrong's World Wide Church of God proclaims the End including the rapture of devoted followers. Armstrong proclaims himself as the long-awaited Messiah.	Space Brothers, super aliens, are scheduled to remove Ufologists, the Light Affiliates, just before the earth is scheduled for demolition.
1914, 1915, 1918, 1923, 1925, 1975	1917	c. 1935	1936, 1943, 1972, 1975	1969

Countdown to the End

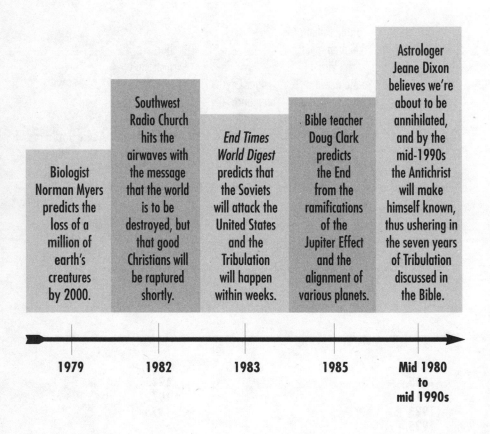

Biologist Norman Myers predicts the loss of a million of earth's creatures by 2000.

Southwest Radio Church hits the airwaves with the message that the world is to be destroyed, but that good Christians will be raptured shortly.

End Times World Digest predicts that the Soviets will attack the United States and the Tribulation will happen within weeks.

Bible teacher Doug Clark predicts the End from the ramifications of the Jupiter Effect and the alignment of various planets.

Astrologer Jeane Dixon believes we're about to be annihilated, and by the mid-1990s the Antichrist will make himself known, thus ushering in the seven years of Tribulation discussed in the Bible.

1979   1982   1983   1985   Mid 1980 to mid 1990s

Countdown to the End

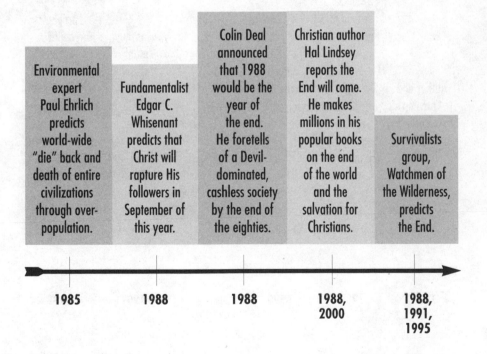

Environmental expert Paul Ehrlich predicts world-wide "die" back and death of entire civilizations through over-population.	Fundamentalist Edgar C. Whisenant predicts that Christ will rapture His followers in September of this year.	Colin Deal announced that 1988 would be the year of the end. He foretells of a Devil-dominated, cashless society by the end of the eighties.	Christian author Hal Lindsey reports the End will come. He makes millions in his popular books on the end of the world and the salvation for Christians.	Survivalists group, Watchmen of the Wilderness, predicts the End.
1985	1988	1988	1988, 2000	1988, 1991, 1995

Countdown to the End

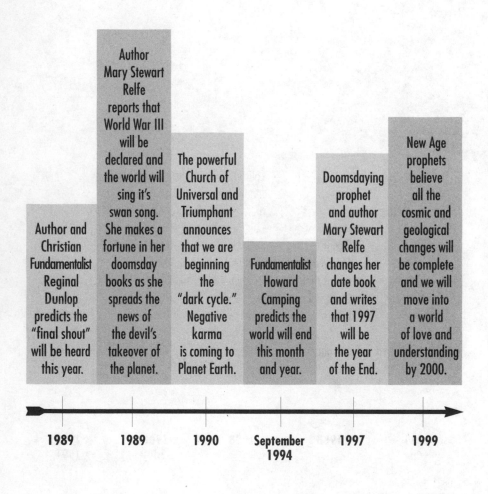

Author and Christian Fundamentalist Reginal Dunlop predicts the "final shout" will be heard this year.

Author Mary Stewart Relfe reports that World War III will be declared and the world will sing it's swan song. She makes a fortune in her doomsday books as she spreads the news of the devil's takeover of the planet.

The powerful Church of Universal and Triumphant announces that we are beginning the "dark cycle." Negative karma is coming to Planet Earth.

Fundamentalist Howard Camping predicts the world will end this month and year.

Doomsdaying prophet and author Mary Stewart Relfe changes her date book and writes that 1997 will be the year of the End.

New Age prophets believe all the cosmic and geological changes will be complete and we will move into a world of love and understanding by 2000.

| 1989 | 1989 | 1990 | September 1994 | 1997 | 1999 |

Countdown to the End

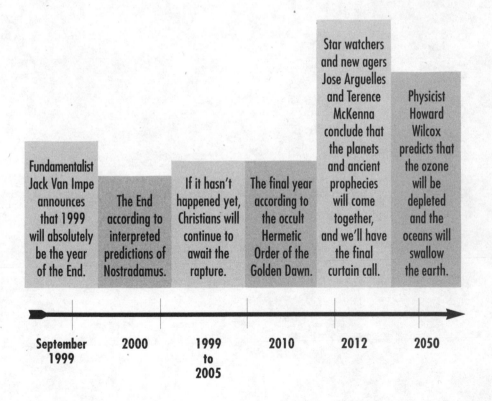

| Fundamentalist Jack Van Impe announces that 1999 will absolutely be the year of the End. | The End according to interpreted predictions of Nostradamus. | If it hasn't happened yet, Christians will continue to await the rapture. | The final year according to the occult Hermetic Order of the Golden Dawn. | Star watchers and new agers Jose Arguelles and Terence McKenna conclude that the planets and ancient prophecies will come together, and we'll have the final curtain call. | Physicist Howard Wilcox predicts that the ozone will be depleted and the oceans will swallow the earth. |
| September 1999 | 2000 | 1999 to 2005 | 2010 | 2012 | 2050 |

APPENDIX A

BIBLIOGRAPHY

Allman, William F. "Fatal Attraction: Why We Love Doomsday," *U.S. News & World Report*. April 30, 1990, p. 12.

Alnor, William M. *Soothsayers of the Second Advent*. Old Tappan, New Jersey: Fleming H. Revel, 1989.

Arguelles, Jose. *The Mayan Factor*. Santa Fe, New Mexico: Bear & Co., 1987.

Armstrong, Herbert W. *The Wonderful World Tomorrow—What It Will Be Like*. New York: Everest House, 1979.

Asimov, Isaac with Frederik Pohl. *Our Angry Earth*. New York: Tor, 1991.

Berkowitz, Bill. *Community Dreams*. San Luis Obispo, California: Impact Books, 1984.

Besant, Anne. *Is Theosophy Anti Christian?* London: Theosophical Publishing Society, 1901.

Blavatksy, H. P. *The Key to Theosophy*. 1889. Pasadena, California: Theosophical University Press, 1972.

Breese, David. *Know the Marks of Cults*. Wheaton, Illinois: Victor Books, 1984.

Brookes, James J. *Maranatha or the Lord Cometh*. St. Louis: Edward Bredell, 1878.

Boyer, Paul. *When Time Shall Be No More: Prophecy Belief in Modern American Culture*. Cambridge, Massachusetts: Harvard University Press, 1992.

Campbell, Bruce F. *Ancient Wisdom Revived: A History of the Theosophy Movement*. Berkeley: University of California Press, 1980.

Carmody, Denise L., Ph.D., and John T. Carmody, Ph.D. *Ways to the Center*. Belmont, California: Wadsworth, 1993.

Carroll, Lee. *Kryon, the End Times—New Information for Personal Peace*. Del Mar: Kryon Writings, 1993.

Carter, Mary Ellen. *My Years with Edgar Cayce*. New York: Warner Books, 1974.

Catechism of the Catholic Church. Liguori, Missouri: Libreria Editrice Vaticana, Liguori Publishers, 1993.

Chandler, Russell. *Doomsday.* Ann Arbor, Michigan: Servant Publications, 1993.

—*Understanding the New Age*. Dallas, Texas: Word, 1988.

Chapman, Clark R. and David Morrison. *Cosmic Catastrophes*. New York: Plenum Press, 1989.

Cohn, Daniel. *Waiting for the Apocalypse*. Buffalo, NY: Prometheus, 1983.

Cohn, Marc. "Hunger 1993," Bread of the World Institute.

Cohn, Norman. *In Pursuit of the Millennium*, 2nd ed. New York: Harper Torchbooks, 1961.

Crim, Keith, general ed. *Abingdon Dictionary of Living Religions*. Nashville, Tennessee: Abingdon Press, 1981.

Cross, F. L., D.Phil., D.D., ed. *Oxford Dictionary of the Christian Church*. London: Oxford University Press, 1966.

Deloria, Vine Victor, Jr. *God is Red*. Golden, Colorado: Fulcrum, 1973.

DeMar, Gary. *Last Days Madness: The Folly of Trying to Predict When Christ Will Return*. Brentwood, Tennessee: Wolgemuth & Hyatt, 1991.

Dixon, Jeane and Rene Noorbergen. *My Life and Prophecies*. New York: Bantam Books, 1970.

Dobson, Rev. Ed, Rev. Ed Hindson and Rev. Jerry Falwell. *The Fundamentalists Phenomenon*. Grand Rapid, Michigan: Baker Book House, 1986.

Dunlop, Reginal. *On Borrowed Time*. Nashville, Tennessee: World Bible Society, 1988.

Eddy, Mary Baker. *Science and Health with Key to the Scriptures*. Boston: Trustees Under the Will of Mary Baker G. Eddy, 1875.

Ehrlich, Anne H. and Paul R. Ehrlich. *Earth*. New York: Franklin Watts, 1987.

Erdoes, Richard. *AD 1000: Living on the Brink of Apocalypse*. San Francisco: Harper & Row, 1988.

Festinger, Leon, Henry W. Reicken and Stanley Schachter. *When Prophecy Fails*. New York: Harper Torchbooks, 1964.

Gallup, George, Jr. and Jim Castelli. *The People's Religion*. New York: Macmillan, 1989.

Gore, Al. *Earth in the Balance*. Boston: Houghton Mifflin, 1992.

Graham, Billy. *Approaching Hoofbeats: The Four Horsemen of the Apocalypse*. Dallas, Texas: Word, 1983.

Gribbin, John R. and Stephen H. Plegemann. *The Jupiter Effect Reconsidered*. New York: Random House, Vintage, 1982.

Grosso, Michael. *Frontiers of the Soul*. Wheaton, Illinois: Theosophical Publishing House, 1992.

Guiley, Rosemary Ellen. *Harper's Encyclopedia of Mystical and Paranormal Experience*. New York: HarperCollins, 1991.

Gaverluk, Emil and Patrick Fisher. *Fiber Optics: Eye of the Antichrist*. Oklahoma City: Southwest Radio Church, 1979.

International Health Watch Report, May/June 1992.

Johnston, Francis. *Fatima: The Great Sign*. Rockford, Illinois: Tan Books, 1980.

Kurtz, Paul. *Transcendental Temptation*. Buffalo, New York: Prometheus Books, 1991.

Larson, Bob. *Larson's New Book of Cults*. Wheaton, Illinois: Tyndale House, 1989.

Lewis, David Allen. "Unidentified Flying Objects: End Times Deception," *Prophecy Intelligence Digest 5*, no.1. David Lewis Ministries, Inc., 1991.

Lightner, Robert P., Th.D. *The Last Days Handbook*. Nashville, Tennessee: Thomas Nelson Publishers, 1990.

Lindsey, Hal with C. C. Carlson. *The Late Great Planet Earth*, rev. ed. New York: HarperPaperbacks, 1992.

Marrs, Texe. *Millennium*. Austin, Texas: Living Truth Publishers, 1993.

Martin, Malachi. *The Keys of This Blood*. New York: Simon & Schuster, 1990.

Mather, Rev. George and Rev. Larry A. Nichols. *Dictionary of Cults, Sects, Religions and the Occult*. Grand Rapids, Michigan: Zondervan, 1993.

Naisbitt John and Patricia Aburdene. *Megatrends 2000*. New York: William Morrow, 1990.

Nelan, Bruce. "Formula for Terror," *Time*. August 19, 1994, p. 47.

Nichol, Francis D. *The Midnight Cry*. Tacoma Park, Washington, D.C.: Herald Publishing, 1944.

Noorbergen, Rene. *Invitation to a Holocaust: Nostradamus Forecasts World War III*. New York: St. Martin's, 1981.

Otis, George, Jr. *The Last of the Giants: Lifting the Veil on Islam and the End Times*. Grand Rapids, Michigan: Fleming H. Revel, Chosen, 1991.

Relfe, Mary Stewart. *When Your Money Fails*. Montgomery, Alabama: Ministries, 1981.

—*The New Money System*. Montgomery, Alabama: Minstries,1982.

Robb, Stewart. *Prophecies on World Events by Nostradamus*. New York: Ace, 1961.

Ross, Ross. *Three Ways of Asian Wisdom*. New York: Simon & Schuster, 1966.

Rubinsky, Yuri and Ian Wiseman. *A History of the End of the World*, New York: Quill, 1982.

St. Clair, Michael J. *Millenarian Movements in Historical Context*. New York: Garland, 1992.

Scallion, Gordon Michael. Earth Changes Report, Matrix Institute.

Schwartz, Hillel. *Century's End*. New York: Doubleday, 1990.

Sears, C. E. *Days of Delusion—A Strange Bit of History*. Boston: Houghton Mifflin, 1924.

Shearman, Hugh. *Modern Theosophy*. Adgar, India: Theosophical Publishing House, 1952.

Symonds, John and Kenneth Grant, eds. *The Confessions of Aleister Crowley, an Autobiography.* London: Routledge & Kegan Paul, 1979.

Teresi, Dick and Judith Hooper. "Last Laugh?" *Omni*, January 1990, p. 84.

Timms, Moira. *Beyond Prophecies and Predictions*. New York: Ballantine Books, 1994.

Toye, Lora Adaile. *New World Atlas*. Socorro, New Mexico: Seventh Ray Publishing, 1991.

Walker, Barbara G. *The Woman's Encyclopedia of Myths and Secrets*. New York: HarperCollins, 1983.

Warlow, Peter. "Reversing the Earth," a report, 1982.

Weber, Timothy P. *Living in the Shadow of the Second Coming: American Premillennialism 1875-1925*. New York: Oxford University Press, 1979.

Whisenant, Edgar. *88 Reasons Why the Rapture Will be in 1988*. Nashville: World Bible Society, 1988.

White, John. *Pole Shift*. New York: Doubleday 1980; ARE Press, 1990.

White, Timothy. *A People for His Name: A History of Jehovah's Witnesses and an Evaluation*. New York: Vantage Press, 1967.

Wilcox, Howard A. *Hothouse Earth*. New York: Prager, 1975.

Woodroff, Sir John, translator. *Mahanirvanatantra*. New York: Dover Publications, 1972.

Zamora, Lois Parkinson, ed. *The Apocalyptic Vision in America*, Bowling Green, Ohio: Bowling Green University Popular Press, 1982.

APPENDIX B

The Eve of Destruction is well documented in fiction and films. To take the quest a step further, you may want to check out the following, often found in libraries and used bookstores.

FICTION

Balmer, Edwin. *After Worlds Collide*, Lippincott, 1950.

A combined edition of: *When Worlds Collide*, and its sequel, *After Worlds Collide*, first published in 1933 and 1934, respectively.

In the first volume, scientists discover that this planets is going to be destroyed by a collision with one of two other planet approaching through space. The only hope is to migrate to the other new planet. The story describes the construction of a spaceship, the destruction of the earth, and the journey through space of a small group of survivors. The second volume continues the story of the survivors on the new planet.

When Worlds Collide "is cleverly spun, in a nervous, almost heretic style, and is saved from the ridiculous by a considerable skill in characterization. Despite its pseudo-science, its crudities, discrepancies, contradictions, inconsistencies and incredulities, it will doubtless hold the attention of many readers who enjoy finding thrills in nightmarish tales." —**New York Times Book Review**

Bear, Greg. *Eon*, Bluejay Books: 1985.

This novel begins with the appearance of a potato-shaped asteroid in orbit around the earth. Early investigation shows that the asteroid is artificial and hollow. Explorers enter the apparently deserted craft and find two mysteries: libraries which contain such earthly classics as *The Adventures of Huckleberry Finn* and *Crime and Punishment* with imprint dates from the future and a series of hollow chambers, the seventh of which continues on without end. Investigation turns up a description of a nuclear holocaust described as taking place in the distant past, which coincidentally is also in the very near future for the explorers. Naturally, the issue becomes whether humans can prevent this catastrophe.

This is a "re-creation of a mythical new civilization on a voyage of discovery. Bear poignantly enacts earth's destruction and spiritual rebirth amongst the advanced residents of the Stone. The many choices facing the survivors provide a clever conclusion to a spellbinding, atmospheric work." —**Booklist**

Bear, Greg. *The Forge of God*, Doherty Associates: 1987.

Three geologists discover an alien artifact in Death Valley and set off a chain of events leading to the discovery that the Earth is about to be invaded by two alien races. One race sends out planet-wrecking machines. . .the other race seeks to enlist the survivors of humanity in tracking down and destroying the planet wreckers.

"The battle over Earth is seen through the eyes of a large cast of well-drawn characters, crowned by a climax of enormous power." —**Booklist**

Butler, Octavia E. *Survivor*. Doubleday 1978.

The title character is Alanna Verrick, a wild human adopted by Missionaries and carried to a distant planet occupied by the warring Gharkohn and Tehkohn tribes. The missionaries are devoted to spread the sacred God-image of humankind; they find the hair-covered humanoid Kohn repulsive, and naturally they choose to side with the wrong tribe, considering both more animal than human.

"Too late they discover just how human the kohn are, human enough to breed with Earthings," **Best Sellers**. "The suspense keeps the reader interested and the satire is effective," —**Library Journal**

Butler, Octavia E. *Dawn*. Warner Books: 1987.

In this first volume in the Xenogenesis trilogy, a band of nuclear holocaust survivors is in the hands of an alien race that offers to save them. The price is high, though: the survivors must participate in the evolution of the aliens by bearing children that incorporate some of the aliens' characteristics.

"Butler is one of the few SF writers who can handle effectively a slow-moving plot that emphasizes characters' emotions. Her command of the language is superior, and her aliens are quite convincing creations." —**Booklist.**

Butler, Octavia E. *Adulthood Rites*. Warner Books: 1988.

In the second novel in the Xenogenesis trilogy, the alien Oankali have rescued the dying remnants of humanity after Earth's nuclear war. Now, though, the children of the two races, called constructs, are resented and feared by the original survivors. This is the story of one such construct, Akin, who possesses an adult mind and voice before he is two years old. Stolen by a barren human community, he grows up knowing both races.

Butler, Octavia E. *Imago*. Warner Books: 1989.

The concluding volume of the Xenogenesis trilogy considers a post-holocaust humanity whose only chance for survival is to be absorbed by the alien Oankali. Totally uninterested in domination, this race thrives on a symbiosis that Earthlings find difficult to credit. That distrust hampers the narrator, a ooloi (neuter) named Hodahs, as it tries to find life partners in the same ratio as its five parents: a human couple, an Oankali couple and itself, the essential ooloi who joins all five and melds their genetic legacy.

"Butler's achievement here is less the abstract reassignment of sexual roles than a warmth and urgency that dramatizes and personalizes these conflicts and transformations." —**Publishers Weekly**

Malamud, Bernard. *God's Grace*. Farrar, Straus & Giroux: 1982.

God has allowed a violent, insufficient humankind to incinerate itself at last. "No Noah this time, no exceptions, righteous or otherwise," He warns Calvin Cohn. But Cohn—paleologist and rabbi's son—inexplicably lives on for now, shipwrecked on an island with Bux, an experimental chimpanzee capable of speech. Soon others appear: chimps, baboons and a lone gorilla. Cohn tries to civilize them better than man, and even to beget an improved human-chimp race that will cause God to love His creation again. His hopes seem to develop, then go awry.

"This is an odd, fanciful book, a mixed bag of surprise characters and enchanting emotions that sometimes jar alongside unlikely happenings and obvious artifice." —**New York Times Book Review**

Percy, Walker. *Love in Ruins: the adventures of a bad Catholic at a time near the end of the world*. Farrar, Straus & Giroux: 1971.

An extravaganza with a Southern setting is a satire on pseudo-profound novels and a sardonic commentary on the bogging down of religion, culture, and interracial, intergroup and interpersonal relationships in the not-too-distant future. The narrator is one Dr. More, descendant of Sir Thomas

More, who believes he had invented a device that will analyze and cure the woes of society.

"A beautifully comic and humane work, the satirist's projection of a grotesque future world based on the realities of the present and stimulus to thought and evaluation and hopefully, to improvement. Percy's style shows mastery of language." —Choice

Pohl, Frederik. *Black Star Rising.* Ballantine: 1980.

In the 21st century, after Russia and the United States have destroyed each other in a nuclear exchange, Castor Pettyman, a rice farmer from the Chinese-ruled American South, becomes a key figure when aliens enter the Solar System making fearful demands. Within its tongue-in-cheek context, this novel utilizes two of the tried-and-true themes of contemporary SF—the young man coming of age and the world turned upside down.

"While Pohl's latest is somewhat predictable, it does contain enough good writing and the author's usual quota of zany (if undeveloped) ideas to ensure agreeable reading." —Booklist

Pohl, Frederik. *The Cool War.* Ballantine: 1981.

Set in the energy-poor world of the early 21st century, this is the story of the Reverend Hornswell Hake, who finds himself drafted by a nameless government agency to serve in the secret "cool war" of subtle, untraceable sabotage; dirty tricks which lower productivity and the quality of life—such as infecting European factory workers with a new strain of flu. But he is also courted, and eventually converted by Leota Pauket, an underground activist fighting to find a way of exposing and stopping the covert strife.

"The author blends an unfailing sense of humanity with biting socio-political commentary to portray a man of the cloth becoming an unwitting James Bond, involved in international dirty tricks that he barely understands." —Library Journal

Pohl, Frederick. *Jem.* St. Martin's Press 1979.

A new planet is ripe for exploitation by Earth's three power blocks: food-exporting nations, oil-exporting nations and people's republics. Three species of intelligent natives enter into appropriate associations with the three colonizing groups, and are thus drawn into the web of conflicts and compromises that reproduces all the evils of earth's politics.

"A cynical ideological counterweight to stories of human/alien cooperation." —Anatomy of Wonder

Pohl, Frederick and Jack Williamson. *Land's End*. Doherty Associates: 1988.

A cosmic disaster destroys the surface of the earth and awakens a sleeping alien menace whose purpose is to assimilate all surviving life into itself.

"Two veteran SF authors combine their storytelling abilities to create a sprawling, complicated SF story." —**Library Journal**

Shute, Nevil. *On the Beach*. Morrow: 1957.

A classic. In 1963 in Melbourne, Australia, people are gradually coming to accept the fact that their death is imminent. The results of an atomic war have wiped out all life in the Northern Hemisphere and the infection is moving southward. The story deals with the way these people face the inevitable end.

"I believe *On the Beach* should be read by every thinking person. Nevil Shute has done an unusually able and imaginative job in depicting how the people might act if there were a radioactive holocaust such as he envisages." —**New York Herald Tribune Books**

West, Morris L. *The Clowns of God*. St. Martin's Press: 1900.

This novel takes place in the last decade of the twentieth century. As the story opens, Jean Marie Barette, lately Pope, has been forced in abdication because the cardinals don't know how else to cope with his apocalyptic visions of the approaching end of the world, and the second coming of Jesus Christ. What follows concerns his efforts to find a way to proclaim his vision without sending his cherished world into a tailspin of chaos and hysteria.

"The fugitive ex-Pope posits all the fearful questions about life that have perplexed us since Hiroshima. West's ultimate answers will disturb some and be dismissed by others, but no one will be left unmoved. The sheer power of his prose and his keen understanding of human nature make this novel a stunning accomplishment." —**Library Journal**

Wyndham, John. *The Day of the Triffids*. Doubleday: 1951.

The radiation from a spectacular meteor shower leaves most of the population blinded. The thin veneer of civilization disintegrates rapidly and is replaced by a quasi-feudal and brutal social order. The Triffids, mobile meat-eating plants, run amok, adding to the danger. Although threatened by the Triffids, the people are their own worst enemy. The plot is effective as a social statement about Western society.

FILMS

The following films, some available on video, deal with topics covered in the book. For instance *On the Beach* concerns the trauma faced when a group knows that they will die shortly from nuclear fallout. In *Defending Your Life* the protagonists attempt to justify actions in their lives as they meet their Judgment Day. A good movie and video guide will help in locating movies that can be used to supplement the text.

Additionally, the *Film Encyclopedia of Science Fiction*, by Phil Hardy (William Morrow & Co., Inc., 1984) provides condensed accounts of all SF movies, from Arthur C. Clarke to Jules Verne, including spectacular Russian science fiction and classics like *Metropolis*, and is an excellent resource for films on Doomsday. *Magill's American Film Guide* can also be helpful in tracking down a specific title.

RELIGION AND SPIRITUALITY

Ark of Noah
Christopher Columbus
Defending Your Life
Fatima: Hope of the World
God Has No Grandchildren
Billy Graham: Hot to Get into the Kingdom of Heaven
Billy Graham: Road to Armageddon
Jesus Then and Now: The Spirit of the New Age
Jesus Christ Superstar
King of Kings
The Lost Years of Jesus
Made in Heaven

Out on a Limb
The Rapture
The Robe
St. John in Exile
The Ten Commandments
War of the Worlds

SCIENCE FICTION

Alien, Aliens, Aliens[3]
Closer Encounters of the Third Kind
The Day the Earth Stood Still
Destination Moon
Forbidden Planet
Invasion of the Body Snatchers
Omega Man
Planet of the Apes
Soylent Green
Space Children
Them!
2001: A Space Odyssey
War of the Worlds

NUCLEAR WAR

Hiroshima, Mon Amour
Kiss Me Deadly
On the Beach

Roman Catholics, 37-39, 90-94,
103-104, 129-131
Russell, Charles Taze, 10, 70-73

S
St. Ambrose of Milan, 37
Salvation, 119-121
Sargent, Abel, 61
Scallion, Gordon Michael, 136-137
Second Coming, 8-11, 37-39, 42,
114-117, 122-127
Seventh Day Adventists, 69, 70
Smith, Joseph, 73-76
Solomon, Paul, 137

T
Taylor, Charles, 131-134
Time line to the end, 216-221
Timms, Moira, 137
Toye, Lora Adaile, 139-141

U
Unidentified Flying Objects, 90,
141-147, 150

V
Van Impe, Jack, 131

W
Wallace, Baird, 146-147
Weather changes, 170-173
While, Ellen B., 70
Wilkinson, Jemima, 61
World Evacuation Project, 145
World Wars, 87-105
Worldwide Church of God, 99-100